CHANGE
and Other Plays

CHANGE
and Other Plays

Wolfgang Bauer

Introduction by Martin Esslin

A MERMAID DRAMABOOK

 Hill and Wang   New York

A DIVISION OF FARRAR, STRAUS AND GIROUX

Contents

INTRODUCTION
The Absurdity of the Real

Wolfgang Bauer, born in 1941 in Graz, belongs to a group of remarkably talented writers who came to the fore in the sixties. Graz, Austria's second city, the capital of the federal province of Styria, has never enjoyed a reputation as the home of a daring young avant-garde. In fact, it has usually been regarded as the place where army officers and bureaucrats go into retirement after being pensioned off: Pensionopolis has always been the city's nickname. And yet it is here that Austria's brightest talents are now blossoming—Peter Handke, Peter Turrini, Harald Sommer, Wolfgang Bauer. They all started here and published their first work in the periodical *Manuskripte*, the organ of the Forum Stadtpark, a remarkable literary and artistic youth center housed in a pavilion in the city's public park.

As different as all these writers are, they have one thing in common: a truly devastating, iconoclastic determination to break with the cant and cliché of the past. If Handke—the only one among them to have made, as yet, any impact in the English-speaking world—devotes one of his plays to an *Assault against the Audience*, Bauer's whole oeuvre must be considered an assault against the traditional theater as well as the audience who frequents it. In his one-acter *Party for Six*, he deliberately mocks the audience's voyeuristic tendencies by promising them the spectacle of erotic incidents at a students' party, and then not showing the party itself, merely the entrance hall to the apartment, through which the participants occasionally pass on their way to the john. In its outward form Bauer's writing seems not only realistic but ultra-realistic. His language—and this, obviously, is an untranslatable element—is the Austrian vernacular, an idiom as earthy and downright rude as it is removed from the polite standard German of the conventional Austrian or German theater. In this respect it can be asserted that Bauer reproduces the movement toward the vernacular, as it is actually spoken, with all its tautologies and repetitions, that Harold Pinter initiated in England. But, unlike Pinter, Bauer is far from being a playwright of mood and subtle atmospheric effects. His is a directness and swiftness of movement that gains its peculiar impact through violent shifts of mood.

Violent shifts of mood, frantic attempts at movement, which, in the end, leave everything as it is. There is a deep pessimism in Bauer's—and his whole Austrian generation's—view of the world. These are the sons of the soldiers of the Second World War, disillusioned, bereft of beliefs or aims. Their fathers may have dreamed of being members of a vast empire from the Urals to the Atlantic Ocean; the sons have grown up in a small country, prosperous enough, but resigned to an existence without excitement—boredom in comfort.

Young people at home, bored, asking: "What shall we do this afternoon? How shall we pass the time?" That is the archetypal starting point of Bauer's plays. The outside world, the world where exciting things still happen, is often represented by English or American pop music, English or American movies. Bauer even has a preference for giving his plays English titles—*Magic Afternoon, Party for Six.* American comic books, Beatles records, English and American detective stories—these are the material of the mythology of the generation he both represents and portrays.

His theater, therefore, might be regarded as an attempt to produce pop art in drama. His contempt for traditional concepts of "high" art is immense. I once took part in a television panel discussion on the future of the theater with him. Eminent experts from all over Europe were arguing at length about the aesthetics, the social function, the political commitment, the poetic possibilities of drama. Bauer, cherubic, round-faced, longhaired, a young Falstaff, sat smiling through the entire proceedings. Finally the moderator asked him for his contribution: "What do you, Mr. Bauer, think the theater needs today?" Bauer merely uttered three words: "More *bad* plays!"

Yet his own plays are far from bad. Their utter rejection of accepted canons of taste, their exuberant abandonment of convention, and their overflowing vitality belie, through the force of the sheer enjoyment in the creative process they reveal, the pessimism and ennui which are their ostensible subject matter. This seems to me the essence of the existential attitude of Bauer's generation of young writers: they are aware of the emptiness and senselessness of their situation—but they see its humorous side; their optimism is the obverse side of their pessimism. Hence the horrors of existence are faced casually, with a grin. So long as one can avoid solemnity, all is well, however black things might be.

This, in many ways, resembles the stance of playwrights of an earlier generation: Beckett and Ionesco above all. They too saw the hopelessness of the human situation; they too replied with humor. But they were more consciously artistic; they transposed their vision into a world of their own, harshly reduced to essentials in the case of Beckett, fantastic and fantasticated in that of Ionesco. Bauer despises the "pretentiousness" of the consciously artistic and finds such transposition unnecessary. For him it is enough to depict reality as it is, suitably coarsened or satirically heightened, but without any of the adornments of "art." In one of his plays (less successful than the others, in my opinion, but nonetheless significant in revealing the author's attitude), his hero is a playwright who has promised a producer a new play by the end of the year. New Year's Eve has arrived, but he has no script. So he arranges a party to which he cunningly invites people who he knows will probably explode when they meet one another. Predictably the party becomes a battlefield. At the end of the evening the playwright hands the producer a number of reels of tape—his new play: life itself has written it for him.

This plot is merely an extrapolation of Bauer's method of composition: he transcribes the situations and characters he finds around him. The bored young people in *Magic Afternoon* and the artists in *Change* are clearly characters he has met and knows intimately. Indeed, I have run across more than one person in the artistic world of Vienna who has assured me that he is the original of one of the characters in *Change*. The incident itself, I am also assured, really happened. Yet whether it did or not, whether the originals of the characters are correct in recognizing themselves in it, seems to me irrelevant. What matters is merely that here a faithful, if foreshortened and heightened, transcription of the boredom and senselessness of real life emerges as a grotesque panorama of the absurdity of existence, existence here and now, in the latter half of the twentieth century.

However impatient of tradition and of the artifices of fine writing he may be, Bauer cannot escape the culture from which he springs and which he has imbibed. (Far from being the child of nature he would like to be taken for, he is a highly educated man and has studied theater history, Romance philology, philosophy, and law at his university.) In their tone and in their language, his plays clearly derive from the great tradition of Austrian folk comedy, of which two of the world's greatest dramatists, Ferdinand Raimund (1790–1836) and Johann Nestroy (1801–62), are the foremost exponents. These men have never enjoyed the international fame they deserved, simply because their linguistic mastery, their brilliant handling of Viennese dialect defies translation. (Thornton Wilder adapted one of Nestroy's plays, *Einen Jux will er sich machen*, as *The Matchmaker*, which later became *Hello, Dolly!* But even Wilder could merely transpose the plot; he could not re-create the verbal fireworks of the original.) The language barrier is equally formidable in the case of Wolfgang Bauer. On the other hand, Bauer's plots are so original that the plays should stand up to translation even if some of the Viennese flavor is lost.

The only way out, here too, is to attempt to transpose not only the text itself but also the geographical location of the action. Writing so deeply rooted in local circumstances can be understood only within a known local framework. As the basic structure of the action of plays such as *Magic Afternoon* and *Change* is truly universal, each performance should endeavor to transfer as much of it as possible to the particular local conditions and use the local vernacular. In this sense the translations offered in this volume should be regarded as a transitional stage between the Austrian original and the final, "relocalized" performance. These plays present a real challenge to regionalism in the theater.

Nor should the surface of brutal directness mislead performers and audiences to think that these plays—and their author—lack a finer sensibility. There is a deep existential anguish behind the grin of cheerful nihilism with which the playwright confronts us. The empty boredom of *Magic Afternoon* which explodes into sudden hatred and violence resembles the mood of *Waiting for Godot*, which it transposes from the stylized expressionist symbolism of Beckett to the coarse neorealism of pop art; and like Beckett's masterpiece, it is, ultimately, the reverse of a cry of despair—an impassioned plea for the courage to face the world as it is and to rebuild a new structure of belief—a new, realistic, existential ethic. Similarly, in the brutal game of manipulation and counter-manipulation in *Change*, we can discern an impassioned appeal for the exercise of human freedom, the abandonment of a view of the world in which man is no more than a manipulated puppet.

The young people of Bauer's generation in Central Europe have become so disillusioned with ideologies, so distrustful of grandiloquent statements, that they would rather die than be caught uttering a generality about beauty, goodness, truth, or justice. They have retreated into a purely negative way of pleading, a secularized "negative theology." Show how horrible the world is and you might shock people into action, rather than lulling them into a complacent feeling of superiority with uplifting political and moral rhetoric.

Some time ago Bauer and a group of friends offered to perform an avant-garde spectacle in a certain small but prosperous Swiss community, in aid of the starving children of Biafra. They collected money for this purpose from the audience and then did nothing more than have a sumptuous meal brought to them on stage, which they devoured with obvious relish. The audience was outraged. But, I believe, they had merely made their point, a valid one, by using their own, and to them the only possible, means—arguing by negatives, direct, brutal, grotesque, absurd, but truly telling because truly shocking.

Martin Esslin

CHANGE

English Version by
Renata and Martin Esslin

Characters

AIR VICE-MARSHAL SIR CHARLES DE MARLIMONT, K.B., D.F.C. (*with Bar*), J.P.

LADY DE MARLIMONT

GEORGIE

FRANK SWANN, *a painter*

BASIL O'MALLEY

HUGH RICHARDS, *an art critic*

SONIA
AMANDA } *night-club hostesses*

ANTOINE, *an art dealer*

TWO POLICE OFFICERS

MR. MIDDLETON

NURSE PEGGY

HOSPITAL DOCTOR

HOSPITAL PATIENTS

HOSPITAL STAFF

SCENE ONE

(*The curtain rises. The stage remains in darkness.* AIR
VICE-MARSHAL SIR CHARLES DE MARLIMONT's *voice is
heard from some way off, the next room but one.*)

DE MARLIMONT
The Pope! . . . That devil, the Pope! The Pope! (*Pause.*)
A whore! You whore, you! Tart! A common tart!
(LADY DE MARLIMONT's *calming voice is heard, but her
actual words cannot be distinguished.*)
(*A key is turned, footsteps, lights. We see a large kitchen,
with all modern fittings and labor-saving devices. There
are two doors: one to the hall, the second to* GEORGIE'S
room.)
(GEORGIE *enters followed by* FRANK. GEORGIE *tosses her
white raincoat into a corner.*)

LADY DE M
(*Calling.*) Is that yououououou?

GEORGIE
(*Mimicking her.*) Yyyyeeeees!

LADY DE M
Are you alooooone?

GEORGIE
(*Smiling at* FRANK.) Noooo!
(LADY DE MARLIMONT *enters. She looks tired and is care-*

*less about her appearance. She wears glasses and an or-
ange-brown dressing gown.*)

LADY DE M
Do you *have* to come home so late?

GEORGIE
Go on, don't run around looking like that . . .
(*She gestures her to leave the room.*)

LADY DE M
Daddy is in a bad way again.

GEORGIE
Is he.

LADY DE M
No peace! I can't get any peace and quiet! Where have you
been all this time?

FRANK
Well, first we went to a movie—

GEORGIE
For Christ's sake, don't talk to her!

LADY DE M
You two get married or else part company! This to-ing and
fro-ing all the time is giving me bad turns. (*To* FRANK.)
After all, you must know *one* day what you want!

GEORGIE
Go on, creep out of here. What *do* you look like!

LADY DE M
Surely, in my own house . . . well, really, that's the limit!

GEORGIE
(*Breaking in.*) Come on, luvey. (*Pushes her out through
door.*) Let's go. Go to your beddie-byes!

LADY DE M
Just you wait!
(*Distant voice:* "*The Pope! That devil, the Pope! You whore, you! Bitch! Tart!*")

FRANK
You don't have to treat her quite so cruelly, do you.

GEORGIE
She drives me crazy, the way she mooches about. She'll keep coming in here, you know how she does: are you alooooone? Is that youououou? Where have you been all this time? And she sings every sentence as if she was doing a solo in a musical. She's quite capable of staying in here and performing her entire repertoire of ancient musical numbers.

GEORGIE
Okay, okay. Give it a rest. I think she's quite sweet.

FRANK
Sweet, my God! When you've got to listen to her day in, day out . . . (*Lights a cigarette.*) Are you going home?

FRANK
I don't know. Do you want me to?

GEORGIE
It's up to you. I'm going to sleep in the kitchen again.

FRANK
What for?

GEORGIE
Do you think I'm going to listen to him raving night after night?

FRANK
The Pope?

GEORGIE

Whore! You whore, you! (*Goes into her room.*)

FRANK

The movie was pretty good, wasn't it, luv? The story wasn't much, but the shots were fabulous . . . the shots of the actual racing, the Monte Carlo ones . . . and the ones at Spa . . . the whole thing, Monza too, don't you think? I wouldn't mind seeing it all again.

(GEORGIE *enters with bedclothes and drops them on the floor.*)

GEORGIE

No chance.

FRANK

Monte Carlo isn't really as good as it looked. . . . Are you going to kip on the floor?

GEORGIE

How about the sink? Get the record player, please.

(FRANK *goes into her room.*)

And something to read—

FRANK

What?

GEORGIE

The latest number of *Jet Set*, with that piece about the College of Fun. I haven't read it yet.

(FRANK *tosses a magazine through the door.* GEORGIE *opens the fridge and helps herself to some yogurt.* FRANK *brings in the record player.*)

FRANK

Can you plug it in here? Oh yeah . . . (*Puts it down.*) Listen, I think I'll stay.

GEORGIE

You'd better go home.

FRANK

Got any beer? Shall we open a can?

(GEORGIE *hands him a can of beer.* FRANK *puts on some soft music, opens can, and pours.*)
(*Doorbell.*)

GEORGIE

Who's that?

FRANK

Better go and see before the old bitch starts up her song and dance again.

(GEORGIE *goes to the door. Voices.* LADY DE MARLIMONT's *voice:*)

LADY DE M

(*Off.*) Georgieieie? Who is it? Georgie, daaarling, who is it?

GEORGIE

It's for me. Stay where you are.

LADY DE M

(*Off.*) Who is it?

GEORGIE

For me! (*Softly.*) Come inside, quick.

(BASIL, RICHARDS, *and* GEORGIE *make a dash for the kitchen.*)

RICHARDS

How do you do, my lord and master.

FRANK

How are things?

BASIL

(*Introducing himself.*) My name is Basil O'Malley.

RICHARDS

Not too bad. Just happened to be passing. . . . Mr. O'Malley wanted to meet you, or rather I wanted you to meet Mr. O'Malley. He is also a painter. (*Winks at* FRANK.) Actually at present he is a locksmith by trade, but he wants to be a painter. A man with a future you might say.

FRANK

Well, sit down. Or lie down.

RICHARDS

Are you two sleeping in the kitchen?

GEORGIE

I am. (*An artificial laugh.*) He is imagining things again. (*Points at* FRANK.)

RICHARDS

Excessive imagination is never a good thing.

GEORGIE

You're not kidding.

FRANK

So what! If you think you're getting a drink, you're wrong.

RICHARDS

Good Lord, no, what do you mean, we're just dropping in.
    (BASIL *is looking through his folder and picks out one or two of his works, muttering "Hhmm."* RICHARDS *points to him.*)
(*To* FRANK.) Well, wouldn't you like to ask Mr. O'Malley what he has got in his folder?

FRANK

Does he always carry all his work around with him?
    (RICHARDS *smiles in the affirmative.*)
May one have a look?

BASIL

(*Looking up.*) I don't know whether you are sufficiently interested in my work.

FRANK

Sufficiently interested, he says.

RICHARDS

Of course our Frankie's interested, aren't you?
(BASIL *chooses a picture.* RICHARDS *indicates to* FRANK: "The greatest dabbler in Christendom.")
Is there enough light?

BASIL

(*Looking around.*) I think it will do. (*Shows the picture.*) "Cedar Trees at Potters Bar."

FRANK

"Cedar Trees at Potters Bar."

BASIL

This is one of my early works . . . this one is better: (*Shows the picture.*) "Cedar Trees at Potters Bar." As you see, I have chosen another aspect here.

RICHARDS

There are two sides to everything. (*Laughs.*)

FRANK

Very good . . . very realistic . . .

BASIL

(*Holding up another picture.*) "Oak Tree Two Miles from Potters Bar."

RICHARDS

Look at that shrub, Frank, there at the back. Doesn't it grab you?

FRANK

(*Laughing.*) Fabulous, Georgie, don't you think?

GEORGIE
Yes, very nice, why shouldn't it be?

RICHARDS
(*Serious.*) We didn't say it wasn't.

BASIL
(*Takes another sketch.*) This one isn't too . . . but this
one: "Group of Elm Trees Three Miles from Potters Bar."
In the left background you can see my bike—it's a Norton
Commander.

RICHARDS
Oh yes—most important.

FRANK
Looks really quite aesthetic.

BASIL
(*Another picture.*) "Trees, Trees, Trees—and Where is
Potters Bar?"

FRANK
Is that the title?

BASIL
It is.

RICHARDS
Where the hell *is* Potters Bar? I can't see anything but trees.

BASIL
Look closely.

GEORGIE
There!

RICHARDS
You don't say! There's a chimney.

FRANK

Splendid. Just like picture puzzles. You could send them to a magazine for a puzzle competition.

RICHARDS

I don't know if our maestro here would agree to that, eh?
(BASIL *smiles, embarrassed.*)

FRANK

What made you take up painting? Did you start all on your own?

BASIL

No, I wouldn't say that . . . I suddenly felt I had to paint!

FRANK

That has been known to happen. (*To* RICHARDS.) Wouldn't you agree, Hugh? It has been known to happen! (*Grins.*)

RICHARDS

The muse seduced him with her iron grip . . . (*Chuckles.*)

FRANK

(*Solemn.*) Paint beautiful trees! She crooned into his ear! (*Laughs.*)

GEORGIE

Christ, how childish can you get!
(BASIL *smiles at her.*)

FRANK

Do you paint anything else but trees?

RICHARDS

Every artist has his hang-up, and with him it's trees. (*Laughs.*)

FRANK

It's really amazing how much is happening among the younger generation.
(BASIL *ties his folder.*)

RICHARDS
Let's go somewhere.

BASIL
How about Ronnie's Place?

FRANK
He knows his way around, doesn't he?

GEORGIE
You can go. I'm going to bed.

FRANK
Do you have to go right now?

GEORGIE
You run along with them!

RICHARDS
At least we should get something to drink.

BASIL
That's true. I'm all for it.

RICHARDS
You get us something, Basil.

BASIL
I don't mind. Where from? What do you want?

RICHARDS
(*Looks around.*) What shall we have?

GEORGIE
Nothing, as far as I am concerned.

FRANK
Couldn't care less.

RICHARDS
Well, let's have a drop of champers, shall we, by way of celebration?

FRANK
Okay.

GEORGIE
Okay, did you say? Don't make me laugh. You're not going out to get some champagne, are you?

RICHARDS
(*To* BASIL.) It's quite simple. You go out of the front door, turn right at the corner, and fifty yards up on the left you'll see a place called Club 77. That's it.

GEORGIE
Will it still be open?

FRANK
Till four in the morning. Give him the key.

BASIL
See you later, then!
    (GEORGIE *goes into the room next door.*)

RICHARDS
Well, what do you think?

FRANK
He's great, that boy.

RICHARDS
Isn't he just?

FRANK
A real gem.

RICHARDS
Since we are in the kitchen . . . is there anything to eat?

FRANK
Hey, Georgie. Could you get Mr. Richards a sandwich or something?

GEORGIE

Okay.

FRANK

What are you doing in there?

GEORGIE

Nothing.

RICHARDS

That chap O'Malley turns up at my local day after day . . . always with his folder, with his pictures . . .

FRANK

Waiting to pounce—

RICHARDS

Waiting to pounce. And when a victim comes along (*Laughs*) he pushes his trees under his nose. One wood after another.

FRANK

No.

RICHARDS

And do you know where he comes from? Potters Bar.

FRANK

I might have known.

RICHARDS

He's really a locksmith. I told you, didn't I? He just dabbles with paints in his spare time. The most ridiculous amateur I've ever come across. And in the evening he tries to lead a great social life. (*Laughs loudly.*) He rides into town on his bike—his Norton Commander, please note—and turns up at my local to meet genuine artists. (*Laughs.*) A regular double existence! A little double-faced Janus head from suburbia.

(*Distant:* "*The Pope . . . The Pope!*")
What's that? The Pope? Someone wants the Pope?

FRANK
That's her father.

RICHARDS
(*Pointing to his forehead.*) He's a bit . . . how awful . . .
(*Distant:* "*The Pope!*")

FRANK
He's great . . .

RICHARDS
Has he got a political thing or something?

FRANK
Sure. He's only got two things on his mind: either the Pope
or he is insanely jealous. He lives under a constant delusion
that the old bitch is deceiving him, the dear old Air Vice-
Marshal!

RICHARDS
Maybe she is?

FRANK
Go on.

GEORGIE
(*Enters in a mini nightdress.*) What do you want to eat?

RICHARDS
What? Well, something, anything you've got. I don't want
to put you out but, I was just saying, since we are going to
camp out in the kitchen any . . .

GEORGIE
I've got three eggs . . .

RICHARDS

Yes, please. (*Smiling at* FRANK.) Two eggs will be fine.
(GEORGIE *sets about preparing the food, at the same time
making more noise than necessary.*)

FRANK

(*Looking through* BASIL's *folder.*) One really should try to
arrange an exhibition with all this.

RICHARDS

Yes, Pop from Potters Bar or something like that.

FRANK

You could write something about him in your paper, some
blown-up interpretation of his tree plantations . . . ?

RICHARDS

One might turn him into some minor Douanier Rousseau
. . . the Customs Officer from Potters Bar! His technique's
good. At least I'll say that for him.

FRANK

Or you could build him up into some great artistic person-
ality.

RICHARDS

How do you mean?

FRANK

Don't you see, what I mean . . . I mean, one could build
him up . . .

RICHARDS

Manipulated man. (*Laughs.*)

FRANK

Right.

GEORGIE

You should be getting on with your work, not talking about manipulating.

FRANK

You know, so that you can say: This is a manipulation by Frank Swann! Not bad, eh?

RICHARDS

And then you stage a gigantic private view where you exhibit him like . . . a pedigree poodle at a dog show.

FRANK

Make a big star out of him.

RICHARDS

That's not very likely. (*To* GEORGIE.) Ah, the eggs are turning . . .

FRANK

You'd have to loosen him up a bit first—

GEORGIE

Hahaha!

RICHARDS

Oh, I don't know.

FRANK

One should guide him so that he will simply do everything you tell him. For instance, kill himself. Everything around him should be . . . organized in such a way that he can't do anything *but* kill himself.

RICHARDS

(*Taking the egg dish from* GEORGIE.) Thank you, (*To* FRANK.) Why go that far? (*To* GEORGIE.) These artists are real sadists.

FRANK

Sadists . . . that reminds me. Can you let me have some bread until the day after tomorrow? (*Laughs.*)

RICHARDS

How much?

FRANK

A fiver will do.

RICHARDS

(*With deliberate generosity.*) First I want to eat this.

FRANK

What do I get if I turn Basil into a real painter?

RICHARDS

(*To* GEORGIE.) He can't get it out of his head!

FRANK

Well, what do I get?

RICHARDS

If he kills himself—a thousand quid.

GEORGIE

Food okay?

RICHARDS

Yes, fine, thanks. I hope he won't be long with the champers.

FRANK

Wouldn't that be the most accomplished murder of all time? Eh? What do you think?

GEORGIE

Very funny!
    (*Footsteps in the hall.*)

RICHARDS

I'm not too keen on the murder angle. But you're right, one might be able to turn that chap into something. The absurd thing about the art world is that, with a bit of promotion, I might well be able to sell our dear old Basil O'Malley.

FRANK

I'll bet you can.

RICHARDS

He is technically perfect, every leaf looks like a photograph. (*Eating.*) Well, I don't suppose anyone will run after his greenery. But suppose he learns to draw people as well as trees. Or at least himself. "Basil O'Malley in a Cedar Wood" . . . or how about "Basil and a Conifer"! (*Laughs.*)

FRANK

That's what I mean. Not bad material, d'you see. To me he is like a canvas, an empty canvas . . .

RICHARDS

A canvas! (*Laughs.*)

FRANK

And I am going to paint on it. That'll be something interesting for a change. But not with a brush and paints . . . (*Painting gesture.*) wishywashy . . . dot, dot, comma, dash, and you've got your face . . . pop art or informal . . . all rubbish . . . all shit . . . no go. O'Malley will have to be manipulated in his entirety . . . that is total art . . . but you'll have to help . . .

RICHARDS

You're becoming fanatic . . .

GEORGIE

His mind's going.

FRANK

Shut up. It fascinates me. At last here's something that really excites me. I suddenly feel enormously productive!

RICHARDS

Only you won't get any bread out of it.

GEORGIE

Right. You tell him that!

FRANK

To hell with bread . . . Oh yes, that fiver you promised me.

RICHARDS

(*Has finished eating.*) Okay. (*Takes out his wallet.*) I've only got three singles. I can hardly give you a ten-quid note.

FRANK

Thanks. That's big of you.

LADY DE M

(*Off.*) You really must call it a day now, it's one o'clock!
    (*The lavatory door is opened and closed.*)

GEORGIE

All right, all right, go to bed!
    (*She puts on a record, softly, turns on a small lamp, and turns off the center light.*)
(*To* FRANK.) Open the window a bit.
    (FRANK *opens the window and looks out.*)

FRANK

Can't see him anywhere.
    (GEORGIE *also looks out. The* AIR VICE-MARSHAL *appears in the doorway in semi-darkness, his head bandaged. He stands, and it is some time before* RICHARDS *notices him.*)

RICHARDS
(*Suspicious*) Good evening, sir.
    (GEORGIE *quickly turns and utters a short cry.*)

DE MARLIMONT
(*In a broken voice.*) Ah, there are the gentlemen . . .
there . . . there . . . in the kitchen . . . a brothel in the
kitchen . . . Where is she . . . where is she? Where is
that whore? Where is the bitch! (*Shakes* RICHARDS.)

GEORGIE
Mummy! It's Daddy! Mummy!

LADY DE M
(*Off.*) I'm in the loo!

DE MARLIMONT
Where is she? Where? Where is the whore? (*He begins to
take crockery from the cupboards and smashes it.*) The
Pope . . . (*Murmurs.*) The Pope . . . Where is she fucking, the old bitch? Where? Where!? Where?

GEORGIE
Mummy loves only you.

DE MARLIMONT
Rubbish, lies.
    (LADY DE MARLIMONT *rushes in.*)

LADY DE M
Come along, Charles . . .

DE MARLIMONT
(*Points to* RICHARDS, *who is smiling at* FRANK.) Who is that?
    (LADY DE MARLIMONT *pushes him out of the kitchen.*)

DE MARLIMONT
Who is that? (*He is pushed outside.*) Who is that gentleman . . .

LADY DE M

Come along, dear, off you go.
(*She closes the door to his room and turns the key. He
bangs against the door. She returns to the kitchen.*)
That's settled it. You'll have to go.

GEORGIE

But we're getting champagne.

LADY DE M

Never mind. I want to get some peace . . .

GEORGIE

But, Mummy . . .

LADY DE M

No "But, Mummy" . . . Off you go . . . please! (*To*
RICHARDS.) You might show a bit of sense, you look a little
more grown up . . .

RICHARDS

(*Rising.*) Are you coming?

LADY DE M

Of course he's coming.

FRANK

Okay. (*Kissing* GEORGIE *lightly on the cheek.*) See you.

RICHARDS

Bye now.

FRANK

Give me a ring tomorrow.

LADY DE M

(*In the kitchen.*) As if one didn't have enough troubles!
You're turning night into day and day into night. And then
you sleep all day.

GEORGIE

Go on, scram.

LADY DE M

Either you get yourself a job next month or you can pack
your bags . . .

GEORGIE

Go on . . .

LADY DE M

I mean it, this time.

GEORGIE

Then you burst into floods of tears and ring everybody up
to find out where I am. Look, why don't you leave me
alone?

LADY DE M

When I was your age I was appearing at the Opera House
in Blackpool as Principal Boy. I had my own car, bought
with my own earnings! You're nothing but a layabout, and
with your father in such a bad way.

GEORGIE

He's only in such a bad way because you've always treated
him badly . . . as if he was dirt . . .

LADY DE M

(*Screams.*) That is not true!

GEORGIE

(*Laughs.*) Why are you screaming, then?

LADY DE M

Because it is not true!

GEORGIE

Don't get excited or your heart will play you up again.

LADY DE M

Just you wait, the good Lord will punish you!

GEORGIE

Don't be such a hypocrite! (*Screams.*) You're only waiting for him to kick the bucket. You're praying for it!

LADY DE M

You wicked bitch, you, if I tell Daddy that . . . you wicked . . . (*Slaps her face.*)
(GEORGIE *hits back. They pull each other's hair.* GEORGIE *pushes her mother out the door and slams it.*)

GEORGIE

Bloody fool!
(*She puts on a record, turns it up loud, and sings in a loud voice.*)
(*A loud whistle outside. She goes to the window, runs to the record player, turns it off, and hurries back to the window.*)
Where have you been all this time?

BASIL

They wouldn't serve me. I went on to Ronnie's Place.

GEORGIE

Everyone's gone.

BASIL

I've got a bottle of vodka. I'll bring it up!

GEORGIE

Okay. (*She goes to open the door.*)

BASIL

(*Enters.*) Got any glasses?

GEORGIE

Hang on, hang on. (*Takes two glasses.*)

(BASIL *puts on record, pours. They drink.* BASIL *begins to laugh.*)
What are you laughing about?

BASIL

(*Pours some more.*) We could make beautiful music together!

(*They drink. He throws himself onto the bedclothes on the floor, whistles to the record.* GEORGIE *closes the window, walks slowly round* BASIL *lying on the floor.*)

CURTAIN

SCENE TWO

(*A boutique called Adam and Eve. Darkness on stage.*
BASIL'*s motorcycle, a Norton Commander, is heard ap-*
proaching. It stops. Footsteps. Someone tries to open a
lock. Sound of scratching and a chisel. Attempts to open
the lock. Hammering. Knocking. Gentle pulling to and
fro of the door for some time. The door opens. Footsteps
on stage—in the stockroom and the boutique.)

BASIL
I'd like to know where the light is.
    (*Light.* BASIL *looks around with pleasure.*)
Come on in! Come on! I wouldn't stop outside.

GEORGIE
You're out of your mind, Basil!

BASIL
What, me? Why should I be out of my mind?

GEORGIE
Turning the light on.

BASIL
Can't see otherwise.

GEORGIE
Breaking in like that! You're mad.

BASIL

After all, I am a fully trained locksmith.

GEORGIE

What if someone comes?

BASIL

Who should come? It's not exactly main shopping hours just now, is it? Four o'clock in the morning. Just the right time of day for shopping.

GEORGIE

Shopping, that's rich!

BASIL

Did you say I was to get myself some new clothes, or didn't you?

GEORGIE

Yes, but I didn't mean it like this. Let's go.

BASIL

You're dead right, I need some new gear. I'm going to stay in town from now on. A painter of my stature has to be trendy. There are some really fabulous things in here. (*Looks around.*) You choose something too!

GEORGIE

You first. I'll tell you if it fits you.

BASIL

What do you mean, fits . . . (*Tries on a jacket and holds a brightly colored shirt against it.*) Pretty cool, eh?

GEORGIE

(*Shyly picks out some green trousers.*) These go with it. (*Studying him.*) Very discreet.

BASIL

(*Shocked.*) Discreet?

GEORGIE

(*Laughing.*) No, of course not. (*Noticing a cap.*) Try this
one! Fabulous! That's great . . .
    (BASIL *admires himself in a mirror.*)

BASIL

Beautiful! I look really beautiful . . .

GEORGIE

Yes—yes, you do!

BASIL

You get yourself something.

GEORGIE

I'm scared.

BASIL

Rubbish, nothing's going to go wrong for me today. I feel
it deep inside me. . . . I feel really good! You know,
pussycat, there are times when I feel really good!

GEORGIE

(*Trying on a midi skirt.*) Look.

BASIL

We'll buy it.
    (*They look around trying things on.*)

GEORGIE

(*Aside.*) Tell me, are you really that keen on me?

BASIL

I'm keen on everything. How do you like this tie?

GEORGIE

Yeah, very nice. . . . Tell me, are you really that keen on
me?

BASIL

How do you mean, "that keen"?

GEORGIE

I'm only asking.
(*Pause. They try on clothes.*)

BASIL

You mean because I've been saying "I love you" all the time?

GEORGIE

Look, does that fit?

BASIL

No. Because I've been saying it?

GEORGIE

That's one of the reasons.

BASIL

(*Puts on jacket and dances in front of the mirror.*) I love you! I love you! I love you! (*Points his tongue.*) Do you know what that means?

GEORGIE

No. (*Tossing a dress aside.*)

BASIL

It's like saying "How do you do," "How do you do," "How do you do," or "Good morning," "Good evening," or "Oh dear," or "How very nice," "very nice," "very nice." It's just something you say.

GEORGIE

I can't figure you out.

BASIL

What you say is immaterial, the main thing is what you experience. You can experience more in one day than others in their whole lifetime. (*Puts on a bathrobe.*) You've got to grab happiness greedily like an octopus! Uuuuuueeeeeh!

(*He moves toward her with the movements of an octopus. She withdraws in surprise, giggling. Finally he embraces her with his tentacles.*)

Uuuuuueeeeeh!

(*She escapes him. He circles round her slowly, bewitching her, making sounds of "Uuuuuueeeeeh."*)

GEORGIE

Don't make so much noise!

(BASIL *makes louder noises.*)

For God's sake, be quiet!

(*He throws her onto the clothes, dances round her, growing softer, making loving sounds, bends over her, chirps like a bird, tickles her. His appearance is threatening, unpredictable, and amusing.*)

BASIL

"I love you!" (*Tickles her.*) Uuuuuueeeeeh!

(*Chirps. Pokes a finger into her stomach. An alarm is heard.*)

GEORGIE

What's that?

BASIL

The alarm. Quick, let's get out of here! (*He picks up as many of the clothes as he can grip.*)

GEORGIE

Leave them!

BASIL

You take some too.

GEORGIE

Leave them, you fool!

(*Tries to pull the clothes away from him.*)

BASIL

Shut up!

GEORGIE

(*Tugging at his clothes.*) Leave them! (*Screams.*) You're mad!

BASIL

(*Throws the clothes on the floor and brutally hits out at* GEORGIE.) Fuck off! (*He picks up the clothes, runs outside, starts up his motorcycle, and rides off.*)

CURTAIN

SCENE THREE

(FRANK's *studio. Early-morning sunlight.* FRANK *and* RICHARDS *look tired, not having been to bed the night before. But they are enthusiastic about their plan. Soft background music.* RICHARDS *is sitting at a table, making notes which seem both to amuse and to fascinate him.* FRANK *is walking up and down. They sip Coca-Cola.*)

RICHARDS
(*Looking out the window.*) I wish I knew how many nights I've wasted like this.

FRANK
(*With enthusiasm.*) It's going to be gigantic, the greatest enterprise ever! Just imagine it—when we've got him where we want him . . . when he's really made it . . . doinggg! we drop him and the reverse mechanism starts up. D'you see? That is to say (a) end of success, I mean lack of success professionally—and then (b) the private mess. That will of course have to be prepared during his successful period, consisting of two aspects: first, love; second, chemistry —that means drugs. In concrete terms: unlucky in love . . . the bird will really have to wear him down. That means she must have a hold over him and at the same time deceive him, intentionally. Everything will have to be carried out with intent and purpose. And then the withdrawal of drugs . . . do you follow?

RICHARDS
Yes.

FRANK
You'll smash him to pieces in your various papers. . . .
We'll influence prospective buyers and collectors in a negative way. That shouldn't be difficult. Antoine, for instance,
will have to be a key figure in this . . . both as a buyer
of pictures and as a pusher of drugs. I'm sure Antoine will
join in, I know the way his mind works, the perverse
bastard . . . He's bored stiff.

RICHARDS
Of course, we'd have to get him to go along with us.

FRANK
That should be a cinch! If necessary, Georgie will have to
come in on it.

RICHARDS
She won't refuse. (*Laughs.*)

FRANK
Oh well, I think it's all over anyway. I don't really care.
We could always start again. (*Grins.*)

RICHARDS
You're being very cool about it, aren't you?

FRANK
What do you mean, "cool"? On the contrary . . . I don't
think Antoine cares for women any more.

RICHARDS
Has he changed horses?

FRANK
Ambidextrous, I think. Listen . . . Antoine will push him
the stuff. That's important to get things moving. A gradual
start with, say, a bit of hash, then the hard stuff, then a few

hypodermics . . . opium . . . it doesn't matter what . . . and then, all of a sudden (*Laughs*) . . . nothing . . . no more to be had. What will he do? He won't go back to Potters Bar. He'll take to drinking (*Laughs*), he isn't good-looking . . . no money . . . no bird will get hooked on him . . . zoing, he does away with himself.

RICHARDS
And what do you get out of it?

FRANK
A thousand quid from you. Naturally I shall have documentary evidence. Everything will be photographed, all the decisive stages in O'Malley's life, including the corpse. I shall write the book to end all books.

RICHARDS
A lot of painters think of writing books. (*Laughs*.)

FRANK
Writing . . . writing is a load of rubbish. I shall be *doing* what those writer chaps write on their shitty bits of paper. I shall actually be doing it. I am manipulating a real life, don't you see?

RICHARDS
I beg your pardon, but I think, in principle, you are not doing anything different from what a writer does. This whole maneuver . . . this murder plot you're working out seems to me . . . seems to me nothing but a kind of . . . oh, what shall I say . . . you want to get something out of your system.

FRANK
For God's sake, don't come that one with me again.

RICHARDS
Your conflict is . . . forgive me . . . the fact that you

have got a conflict but can't write poetry. Maybe that's a
bit exaggerated, I admit.

FRANK

What sort of a conflict have I got anyway?

RICHARDS

What a question!

FRANK

Well, tell me! What sort of conflict?

RICHARDS

Well . . . to start with there is a certain Miss Georgie . . .

FRANK

No! (*Pause.*)

RICHARDS

You've tried suicide twice . . . I don't want to analyze all
this just now . . . you . . .

FRANK

That's very good of you. Don't bother to analyze me, spare
yourself the trouble of an analysis! Your analyses are cen-
tered on your own ego . . . you only see what you want
to see.

RICHARDS

In Basil . . . if I might make one more point . . . in Basil
you want to fuse your two main aims.

FRANK

Which are what?

RICHARDS

Success and death. And since you can't manage to achieve
either of them for yourself, you want to come face to face
with them on another level altogether. And that's all there
is to it.

FRANK
Thank you very much, Mr. Headshrinker.

RICHARDS
But now for my program. The positive side. Look!

FRANK
Let's see.

RICHARDS
Summary: technically I have no complaints about our *objet trouvé* . . . our *objet trouvé manipulé.* (*Laughs.*) So there's just the question of the subject matter . . . to give me the chance of a suitable interpretation. Seeing he's so involved with trees, there are quite a few things I could say about that. Oh, you know . . . the loneliness of modern man . . . all these trees represent people with whom he has no contact, and so on. You'll have to tell him what to paint. As far as promotion is concerned: I shall put two of his sketches into the paper tomorrow. Influential circles will be informed.

FRANK
What about a private view?

RICHARDS
It's too soon for that. First we might have some little scandals. I would suggest . . . stripping at some formal occasion . . . for instance, at that reception the Minister for the Arts is holding. What do you think? That will create quite a ripple . . . television . . .

FRANK
First-class! That's great!

RICHARDS
Or painting other people's cars . . . you get minor sen-

tences for that kind of thing. He'll survive those and rise from the police court like a phoenix from the ashes. Then, of course, there will have to be a private program of education and indoctrination. Books . . .

FRANK

I have that in mind as well. You can undermine his confidence and induce a defeatist mood with the help of the right kind of author and philosopher.

RICHARDS

Introduce him to as many people as possible . . . You know a lot of people . . .

FRANK

Antoine is the most important.

RICHARDS

Yeah—he might be able to move in with him.

FRANK

I'd rather he stayed with me, then I'd have him under my thumb.

RICHARDS

Fair enough. And we'd have to get him hung up on a nice dollybird.

FRANK
Georgie.

RICHARDS

(*Eyes him dubiously*.) You do have a twisted mind! Well . . . (*Pause*.) Tell me, why shouldn't it be you instead? Us do the whole thing to you, I mean. I know why, you wouldn't strip at a reception! (*Laughs*.) (*Pause*.) Well, that's roughly how I see it.

FRANK

(*Pause.*) There's no reason why it shouldn't go very well
. . . (*Puts on a slow record, walks about.*)
   (RICHARDS *stretches.*)

RICHARDS

Ah well, I'm ready for beddie-byes . . . Hell, I've got to
go to the private view at eleven . . .

FRANK

What private view is that?

RICHARDS

Oh, some old master . . . (*Reads the invitation.*) Kenneth
Debenham . . . tut, tut . . .

FRANK

Relative of Freebody's? (*Laughs.*)

RICHARDS

How do I know . . . I've got my job to do . . .

FRANK

D'you want anything to eat?

RICHARDS

Eat? Hm, I think I'll have breakfast at home. After all, I've
got a family . . . Who's that on the record?

FRANK

Don't you know?

RICHARDS

Gerry Mulligan?

FRANK

Right.

RICHARDS

From time to time I like to remember the old ones.

FRANK
I'm turning on to jazz again myself.

RICHARDS
Do you know Joey Smeeton?

FRANK
Yeah . . .

RICHARDS
He's a specialist on the late fifties . . . got stuck there. One of the greatest jazz experts . . .

FRANK
Quite a nice guy. I . . .

RICHARDS
You know . . . jazz . . . Jesus, I can remember when I used to do a talk on jazz every week . . .

FRANK
Those were good days . . .

RICHARDS
There was something going on then . . . enormous enthusiasm . . . the heyday of the avant-garde . . .
    (*Doorbell.* FRANK *goes to open the door.* RICHARDS *rises, puts on his tie, combs his hair.* FRANK *enters with* GEORGIE.)

GEORGIE
Morning.

RICHARDS
Morning.

FRANK
You going?

RICHARDS

Yeah . . . (*Considering what to say*) . . . well, then, maestro . . . we'll leave it like that. I expect I'll meet Antoine at the private view. I can put him in the picture a bit.

FRANK

You do that. Give him my regards.

RICHARDS

Right you are, then. (*Exit.*)

FRANK

Bye now.

GEORGIE

See you.

FRANK

How come you're up so early?

GEORGIE

Me?

FRANK

Yes, you.
    (GEORGIE *laughs.*)

GEORGIE

It's such a lovely day—

FRANK

I haven't had any sleep at all. We've been working on that manipulation.

GEORGIE

(*To herself.*) The what? . . . Has Basil been here?

FRANK

No. Why should he? He doesn't know where I live. I'd like to know, though, where he got to last night.

GEORGIE

Give me a cig.

(FRANK *passes her a cigarette. She gives him a little kiss.*)
How are you, then?

FRANK

Sleepy . . . but otherwise okay. That guy Richards!

GEORGIE

What's he been doing all night?

FRANK

He's worked out the master plan for O'Malley.

(*Shows her the notes. She puts them back.*)
But—and this is typical of Hugh—he had to start talking
about my subconscious. He said I only want to do the
whole thing because I am . . .

GEORGIE

Because that's what you are like.

FRANK

No, not quite like that. Anyway, it doesn't really matter.

GEORGIE

(*Yawning.*) I'm going to lie down for a bit. (*Goes to set-
tee.*) . . . (*Pause.*) You're so stupid . . . why don't you
ask Richards to put some of your work into the paper or try
and get it sold. You're always broke . . . we could get
married . . .

FRANK

Hohohoho . . . you know very well that would be a waste
of time. Come on, honey, we get on much better like this.
This obsession to get married . . . it's . . . it's some ridiculous fixation you've got. (*Shakes his head, walks about.*)
. . . Do you want some coffee?

GEORGIE

No . . . you know very well I don't like coffee!

FRANK

I'd like to know where O'Malley ended up last night.

GEORGIE

(*Laughs.*) Would you really like to know?

FRANK

Why, do you know?

GEORGIE

No. (*Laughs.*) (*Pause.*) Ah well, he came back to my place . . .

FRANK

Back to your place! Why didn't you let me know? You're just playing me up.

GEORGIE

After you'd gone . . . didn't you bump into him?

FRANK

No . . .

GEORGIE

He arrived immediately afterward, along with a bottle of vodka.

FRANK

And then what?

GEORGIE

We finished it up between us.

FRANK

Well? Give me the lowdown—what's he like? I hardly know him.

GEORGIE
Quite nice, actually.

FRANK
You must have got plastered, if you finished off the whole bottle . . .

GEORGIE
(*Shaking her head.*) Well . . . maybe . . .

FRANK
And what else?

GEORGIE
The funniest thing happened this morning.

FRANK
Yes?

GEORGIE
He gets up, gets dressed . . .

FRANK
So you've finally done it!

GEORGIE
You're round the bend.

FRANK
Well, if he had to get dressed?

GEORGIE
Listen. He says: "Let's go." I say: "Where?" He says: "Get some gear." So I say: "You're daft, in the middle of the night?"

FRANK
Seems to me you're more than friendly with him.

GEORGIE
What do you expect after a bottle of vodka!

FRANK
Carry on.

GEORGIE
Do you know where he went?

FRANK
No.

GEORGIE
Guess.

FRANK
Where?

GEORGIE
To the Adam and Eve boutique! He breaks a lock, gets inside, pinches all sorts of tops, pants, shirts . . . God knows what else.

FRANK
Come off it!

GEORGIE
I swear it!

FRANK
And you went inside with him?

GEORGIE
Yes. It was absolutely fascinating! I thought he'd come round to see you.

FRANK
So that's why you are here.

GEORGIE
I thought you'd be interested.

FRANK

Yes, indeed! (*Walks about.*) (*To himself.*) That's good. (*To* GEORGIE.) In any case, you're already included in the plan.

GEORGIE

What do you mean?

FRANK

Well, not quite yet. First he's got to establish himself as a painter. Then you are going to tip the scales.

GEORGIE

You don't say!

FRANK

You see, you are going to present the turning point. You are going to change the course of the spaceship (*Laughs*) . . . you are going to bring the spaceship back to earth.

GEORGIE

I don't know what you are talking about. And I don't care.

FRANK

A hard landing. So you haven't slept with him yet?

GEORGIE

Don't keep asking such idiotic questions.

FRANK

What do you mean, "keep asking"? It's important—yes or no?

GEORGIE

No! But it wouldn't make any difference if I had.

FRANK

Not in this case. But all in good time, sweetheart.

GEORGIE

(*From the sofa.*) Come here.

FRANK
What?

GEORGIE
Come here.

FRANK
(*To himself.*) Exactly! (*Makes a note.*)
  (*Doorbell.*)
(*To* GEORGIE.) Go and open the door, would you?
  (GEORGIE *goes.*)

GEORGIE
Okay. (*Off.*) Hi!

BASIL
(*Off.*) Hail to thee, blushing virgin!
  (BASIL *enters, gaudily dressed, with* GEORGIE.)

FRANK
Hello, there!

BASIL
Hail to thee, hail! I'm thrilled to bits about your tits!
Hahaha! How are you, sir?

FRANK
Don't call me sir. My name is Frank.

BASIL
And mine's Basil.

FRANK
I'm afraid I can't offer you a drink, but—eh, did you have
a good night?

GEORGIE
Breaking in . . .

BASIL

Shopping, you mean! Yes, a stupid affair that. Arose out of necessity, you might say.

FRANK

Great. Cigarette?

BASIL

No thanks. (*Takes out a cigar and lights it.*)

FRANK

I thought you'd gone back to Potters Bar.

BASIL

No, I'm going to stay in town. There's just the question of where I'm going to live.

FRANK

You can stay with me, if you like.

BASIL

(*Pleased.*) Really?

FRANK

But you'll have to get on with your painting. Otherwise it's no fun.

BASIL

(*With exaggeration.*) I shall be a great artist! I shall be indebted to you for evermore.

GEORGIE

Where've you been all this time?

BASIL

Everywhere and nowhere! I've been out and about with my little sweetheart.

FRANK

Sweetheart?

BASIL

My Norton. My Norton Commander. I've been roaring right across town on her. There's nothing better than racing along on my Norton at eighty miles an hour, along the main roads.

FRANK

At this time of day?

BASIL

Right in the middle of the road, in and out of the traffic.
    (GEORGIE *laughs.*)
Toioioinnnng—lovely day today! I must paint something
. . . I simply must.

FRANK

Be my guest. Help yourself to anything you want, whenever you like. (*Puts his arm round* BASIL.) And if you want to know anything, just come and ask me.

BASIL

Got paper and paints?

FRANK

Over there. Help yourself.

BASIL

You mean that?

FRANK

Don't ask silly questions! (*To* GEORGIE.) I can't even remember the last time I was so keyed up to start painting.

BASIL

"Keyed up" isn't the word. I'd like to swallow up the paper!
    (GEORGIE *laughs.* FRANK *laughs.*)

GEORGIE

What are you going to paint?

BASIL
Peace and quiet!

FRANK
A woodland scene, I suppose . . . eh? Are you going to paint a woodland scene?

BASIL
A nude!

FRANK
A nude?

BASIL
A nude . . . what one generally refers to as a nude painting.

FRANK
Have you ever painted a nude model?

BASIL
Painted? I've never actually painted one.

FRANK
Do you mean to paint a nude without a model?

BASIL
Basil can paint nudes without models, even in the dark, if necessary. (*He smiles.*)
    (GEORGIE *smiles too.* FRANK *notices her.*)

FRANK
(*To* GEORGIE.) Pussy, wouldn't you like to sit for him?

GEORGIE
Are you out of your mind?

FRANK
Look, I'm sure Basil would like it if you sat for him, eh?

BASIL

Quiet! I must concentrate!

FRANK

(*To* GEORGIE.) Go on, won't you do it?

GEORGIE

Leave me alone.

FRANK

But it's very important that Basil should learn to paint nudes from live models, sweetheart. (*Playfully pinches her nose.*)

GEORGIE

Go to hell.

FRANK

What? Don't you want to? Come on . . . don't make so much fuss about it. You're not usually so prim . . . (*Begins to undo her dress.*) Come on, take that off . . .

GEORGIE

(*Slaps his face.*) You're behaving like a seventeen-year-old . . .

FRANK

(*Pulls off top half of the dress.*) Look, Basil, look quick . . .

BASIL

Absolute quiet, please.

GEORGIE

(*To* FRANK.) Bloody idiot!

FRANK

(*Putting on a soft record.*) Basil, you tell her to take her clothes off. She's shy with me.

BASIL

(*Vaguely.*) What's that?

FRANK

You tell her.

BASIL

(*Stands up, looks at* GEORGIE *with mock seriousness.*) I think you are being too clumsy about this, Frank. It's got to be done very slowly, very gently, d'you see?

(*Reaches her, starts to undress her slowly.*)
Very gently . . .

(*He whistles in tune with the record.* GEORGIE *stands naked.* BASIL *sits at the drawing board and starts to sing to the record.* FRANK *laughs.*)

CURTAIN

SCENE FOUR

(*Sleazy night club. Curtained-off partitions in the back-ground. It is fairly quiet. A man comes out from behind the curtains, combs his hair, and leaves the club.* SONIA *is at the bar.* AMANDA *and* SUZANNE *are busy behind the curtains. Soft music.*)

AMANDA
(*Emerges, straightens her hair.*) What's wrong? The place is like a morgue tonight.

SONIA
It's Wednesday.

AMANDA
On Wednesdays they all stay at home with their wives.

SONIA
Is that one having another bubbly?

AMANDA
He's not drunk the first half of the bottle. Mean old git!

VOICES
(*From behind curtain.*) Amanda! Amanda!

AMANDA
Okay . . .

SONIA
Go to Mr. Rainer, luv, would you. Suzie is with Mr. Heth-erington. I'll be along in a minute.

AMANDA
Okay.

VOICE
Suzie. Suzie, my love!

AMANDA
Coming . . .
     (BASIL *and* FRANK *enter*.)

SONIA
(*Eagerly*.) Gentlemen!

BASIL
Charmed, I'm sure.
     (SONIA *whistles*.)
Is this a bloody football ground or something?
     (AMANDA *enters*.)

AMANDA
Good evening, gentlemen. Shall we all have a drink inside?

FRANK
No, thanks. We'll stay here.

SONIA
Would you like a long drink, sir? Whisky?

BASIL
Don't you want to go inside, Frankie?
     (FRANK *gestures: not enough money*.)

AMANDA
Step inside, you gorgeous creatures.

BASIL
Hang on a minute, no need to rush things. We'll have a
drink first.

FRANK

Two beers.

(AMANDA *exits.*)

SONIA

Work up a bit of courage, eh?

BASIL

Cut out the small talk, auntie, or I'll knock you flat on the counter.

SONIA

You're an impulsive one.

VOICE

Sonia! Sonia!

SONIA

Coming! Cheerie-bye, milksops! (*Exit.*)

BASIL

What are we here for? We can drink beer anywhere.

FRANK

Not in such pleasant surroundings. I like it here. It inspires me in some way. Cheers!

(*They drink.*)

It's a relaxed setting, that's always important. It comes out in our work, you see?

(*Giggling from behind curtain.*)

BASIL

The giggling of these subhuman creatures turns me over.

FRANK

For Christ's sake, don't use words like "subhumans." You sound like Enoch. You'll have to drop that kind of talk if you want to be a success. We may manage to get you an exhibition in two months' time, okay, but you'll have to watch it, Basil. They'll knock you down just as fast. Above all, remember: be relaxed. Your pictures are too rigid . . . d'you see what I mean, technically they're good, that's okay, some are amusing, but nothing moves, Basil. All the enthusiasm in the world won't help, you've still got a lot to learn. I'm sorry if I'm becoming didactic, but read some Beckett—*Molloy*, for example.

BASIL
Molloy, sounds good.

FRANK
Or *Ulysses* by Joyce, at least the last few chapters . . . or Laurence Sterne . . .

BASIL
D'you think these birds won't do anything for free?

FRANK
Or read *Civilisation* by Sir Kenneth Clark, or *The Painting of Schizophrenics* . . . d'you see. Talent is fine, and you've got talent, but you won't get anywhere without some background. You're not stupid . . .
(AMANDA *enters with an empty champagne bottle.*)

AMANDA
(*To* BASIL.) Gorgeous to look at but so inexperienced! (*Shows him her tongue.*)

BASIL
Hideous to look at and so battered about! If I were you I wouldn't open my mouth so wide. Do you want everyone to see those black stubs of yours you call teeth?

AMANDA
(*Massaging the back of* BASIL'*s neck.*) You rough little bear!

BASIL

(*To* FRANK.) This is too much!
    (AMANDA *goes out with another bottle.*)

FRANK

Or take jazz, you don't know anything about it. Albert
Ayler, Charlie Mingus, have you ever heard of them?

BASIL

No.

FRANK

You've got an enormous backlog of culture to catch up on.
It's all very well to be naïve, it has its advantages. Even in
the field of painting, it has its own fascination. But in the
end you're always the one who's left out in the cold.

BASIL

I'm going in there.

FRANK

Stay here, you haven't got a chance without money, and
anyway I want to talk to you.

BASIL

Listen, Frank. I'm your friend.

FRANK

Of course you are.

BASIL

I can stay with you?

FRANK

Of course you can.

BASIL

I've got to tell you something. All this talk is useless.

FRANK

But . . .

BASIL

Listen, the other night I slept with your . . . what's her name . . .

FRANK

Georgie.

BASIL

I've slept with her.

FRANK

(*Surprised.*) Oh well, that's okay. I thought you had . . .

BASIL

Listen, there's something else. She told me you're planning something, you want to "build me up" . . .

FRANK

Go on . . .

BASIL

She said that I'd end up killing myself. I didn't quite get what she meant. Being in the kitchen, it was all a bit odd. But tell me, is it true?

FRANK

It's quite untrue.

BASIL

What did you have in mind, little Picasso? (*Pinches his nose.*)

(SONIA *comes out.*)

SONIA

Well, made up your mind yet?

BASIL

You think about it! (*To* SONIA.) Let's go, one bottle, please.

SONIA

And one for the other gentleman?

BASIL
He's got some thinking to do.

SONIA
Oh, a proper scholar! (*Laughs.*)
(SONIA *takes a bottle and disappears behind the curtain with* BASIL.)

VOICE
Sonia!

BASIL
(*Off.*) No Sonia for you, my friend!
(FRANK *sits alone, searches for money, puts it on the bar counter.* RICHARDS *enters.*)

RICHARDS
A very good evening, one and all!

FRANK
Hello, Hugh.

RICHARDS
You alone?

FRANK
Basil's in there. (*Points to curtains.*)

RICHARDS
Oh, I see. (*Laughs.*) I suppose he is busy being built up!

FRANK
Well, I think things may turn out harder than we thought.

RICHARDS
He's practicing stripping for tomorrow. (*Laughs.*)

FRANK
I don't know.

RICHARDS
What's the matter with you, what's wrong?

FRANK
What should be wrong?

RICHARDS
Feeling all right?

FRANK
Yeah, I'm feeling all right.

RICHARDS
You don't look it, though. You look as if you were in one hell of a mess.

FRANK
What do you know about my situation . . .

RICHARDS
I know, I've said it before; you're always in the situation that *you think* others think you are in.
 (AMANDA *comes out. A man leaves.*)

AMANDA
So long, Mr. Rainer! (*To* RICHARDS.) Hello there, Hugh my love!

RICHARDS
Hello there, how are you?

AMANDA
What are you drinking?

RICHARDS
Give me something to settle my stomach . . . brandy, I think.

AMANDA
Is your learned friend having one too?

FRANK

No, thanks.

RICHARDS

Give him another beer, Amanda.

AMANDA

Right-ho.
(*Excited voices from behind curtain,* SONIA *and* BASIL.)

SONIA

Why the hell did you order a bottle if you can't pay for it? Get out!

BASIL

Don't be so practical. Just when it's getting cozy.

SONIA

Get out, you git! Get out!
(BASIL *appears.*)

BASIL

What a shambles! Hello, Hugh, you drunken sod.

RICHARDS

What's up?

SONIA

He doesn't want to pay for his drink, the bastard, the shit!

RICHARDS

How much?

SONIA

Eighty-five bob.

BASIL

You don't think I'm going to pay that much, do you? You and your black teeth! You ought to count yourselves lucky to be allowed to touch a lovely man like myself, you slimy toads!

RICHARDS
Silence! (*Pays the money.*) There you are, now shut up.
Come on, Basil. (*Clicks his fingers.*) Amanda! (*To* FRANK.)
Coming to celebrate, Frank?

FRANK
Go away and play.

BASIL
(*Going with* RICHARDS.) Now they're going to get it!

FRANK
What about my beer.

AMANDA
Coming right up, sir!

CURTAIN

SCENE FIVE

(*At* ANTOINE's. *The room is decorated in red velvet. Very distinguished.* ANTOINE *wears a purple velvet smoking jacket. He is arranging some things on a small table: ash-trays, hashish cigarettes, a bowl of punch. A record is playing: Sir John Gielgud in the Storm Scene from* King Lear. *Doorbell.* ANTOINE *goes to the door and opens.*)

ANTOINE
(*Off.*) Let me embrace you, dearest hedgehog.

FRANK
(*Off.*) Hello! Antoine!
  (*They enter.*)

ANTOINE
Rest your weary limbs, m'dear. (*Arranges cushions.*) I've been awaiting you eagerly.

FRANK
Yes . . . well, Georgie and Basil will be here soon.

ANTOINE
Basil . . . (*Giggles.*) I love that name. And how are you, my dear old friend? (*Turns off record.*)

FRANK
All right, thanks.

ANTOINE
As successful as ever?

FRANK

Well, you know, I'm not doing much work just now.

ANTOINE

Well, I must say your last exhibition was absolutely tops. Absolutely tops. Only yesterday I had a friend of mine here from Paris, Pierre Bauer. I showed him your catalogue. He wants to meet you in the next few days and he says it might well be possible to arrange an exhibition for you in Paris, m'dear. You see, your dear old Antoine does for you what he can.

FRANK

Thanks a lot. But just now I've got my mind on other things . . . you know what . . . that's why I'm here.

ANTOINE

Yes. Great! Absolutely first-class! When I heard of your diabolical plan . . . (*Pensive.*) well, I turned a few somersaults inside myself with joy. (*Grins like an old woman.*)

FRANK

Are you with us, then?

ANTOINE

Antoine is always with it, because . . . well, because . . . being with it, being right at the heart of things, is everything. (*Giggles.*) Not just on the edge of things, my dear little hedgehog! (*Stares at* FRANK, *laughs.*) Right . . . (*Rises.*) Now we'll play our private national anthem.

FRANK

The "Pathétique"?

ANTOINE

Indeed. (*Puts on record.*) Now tell me all about that rumpus at the Minister's reception. Did that little rascal really strip?

FRANK

I wasn't there, but it's supposed to have been great. All things considered, the manipulation is going fine—full speed ahead.

ANTOINE

Manipulation—is that what you call it? A real stroke of genius! But tell me, how did you get this—well, you might call it magical idea?

FRANK

It just kind of happened. One thing leads to another. I . . . you know, it's an occupation like any other. (*Smiling.*) Only it's nice and pointless.

ANTOINE

(*After a little hesitation, affecting seriousness.*) Frankie, I can only congratulate you. You are one of the last of those favored beings . . .
   (*Doorbell.*)
   (ANTOINE *goes to open.*)

ANTOINE

(*Off.*) My dear giraffe! Incline your head toward my lips! (*Kiss.*)

GEORGIE

(*Off.*) Hello, Antoine.

ANTOINE

(*Off.*) And that is Basil, the Great!
   (*They enter.*)
May I call you by your first name straightaway? Actually I won't call you Basil. I have this little habit of calling human beings—so called—by animal names. She is my giraffe and Frank is my hedgehog. (*Looks intently at* BASIL.)

BASIL

Hello, Frank!

FRANK

Hello to you!

ANTOINE

And he is going to be my slick little pig! Slickety pig.
  (FRANK *laughs.*)

FRANK

Antoine, you mustn't offend him like that!

ANTOINE

Of course, I may. After all, I am Antoine. (*To* BASIL *and*
GEORGIE.) Recline and rest your bodies in my oh-so-soft
armchairs . . . and have some punch, my dears! Punch,
the drink of the gods!

FRANK

Slickety pig! (*Laughs.*)

GEORGIE

You should laugh with a name like hedgehog.

BASIL

I thought I was going to get hash to smoke. I can wait for
the punch.

ANTOINE

You'll get all your heart desires.

BASIL

And what animal are you?

ANTOINE

Me? I am the highest-ranking power among the animals.
(*Reflects.*) I am the jellyfish. (*Laughs. Passes a cigarette to*
BASIL.) There you are, slickety pig. Draw hard, inhale deep,
and leave it there. Let your lungs burst!
  (BASIL *inhales.*)
How are you, my little giraffe?

GEORGIE

Not too bad, thanks.

(ANTOINE *passes her a cigarette and one to* FRANK. AN-
TOINE *smokes a pipe. Silence while they smoke.*)

BASIL

Smells like in a church.

ANTOINE

Right, slickety pig! It has a lot to do with God, too. Inhale,
my friend! Inhale deep! You've got to inhale hash deep.

GEORGIE

(*To* BASIL.) Do you notice anything?

BASIL

My head is beginning to fill.

ANTOINE

Have some punch, slickety pig! Punch, giraffe! Punch,
hedgehog!

FRANK

Yes, please! (*Pours.*) Basil, tell Antoine what happened at
the reception.

ANTOINE

Yes, please do. Please tell us.

BASIL

How many more times?

ANTOINE

You haven't told me yet, please, slickety pig!

BASIL

Well, there isn't much to tell. I took my clothes off . . .

ANTOINE

Tell it slowly. This has to be savored. Come on, slickety
pig!

BASIL

First of all, I don't like my new nickname.

ANTOINE

All right, you can be a shark!

BASIL

And secondly, I can't stand that dirge.

ANTOINE

That's Tchaikovsky!

BASIL

Tchaikovsky or no Tchaikovsky . . . (*Giggles.*) Tchai-kovsky or . . . or no Tchaikovsky . . . You can stuff this music up your arse. (*Giggles.*)

ANTOINE

Slickety pig, you are offending a god!

BASIL

God is dead . . . there is no God . . .
    (*Rises. The drugs are beginning to take effect.*)
the whole world is . . . (*Giggling.*)

GEORGIE

Beginning to feel something?

BASIL

Some imagination . . . hell . . . Hell is other people . . .

FRANK

(*Casually in time to the music.*) Manipulation . . . (*Whis-tles, winks at* ANTOINE.)

ANTOINE

Tell us, shark! (*Moves to* BASIL, *grips his arm.*) Tell us, shark dear.
    (GEORGIE *starts to giggle.*)
(*To* GEORGIE.) You high?

GEORGIE

My, my! (*Giggles*.)

FRANK

Tell us about the French . . .

BASIL

Well, I came in . . . and there are all the artists . . . all those Michelangelos standing in a line like housewives queueing outside the breadshop.

ANTOINE

Those Michelangelos! How right you are!

BASIL

There I am and I ask them: anything being given away free here? And what do you think they were doing? They were all queueing to see the Minister for the Arts . . . and what do you think they got?

ANTOINE

What?

BASIL

A warm handshake! I mean, a soggy handshake. Because if I shake hands with three hundred people I'm bound to get wet hands. So, I thought, I'll get into line as well . . . I had a look at their faces . . . each one looked more idiotic than the next, and they were all grinning at the Minister . . . they were all . . . ah, now the reefer's beginning to work . . .

ANTOINE

Tell us more! (*Watching* BASIL *intently*.)

BASIL

I get up to him . . . and I say: "*Bon soir, monsieur*." The Minister, quick . . . quick on the uptake thinks I'm French. He says: "*Bon soir, monsieur*." So I say: "Beg your pardon, but I am as British as roastbeef and Yorkshire pudding. I was only pretending."

(ANTOINE *and* GEORGIE *laugh*.)

ANTOINE

(*To* FRANK.) The man's a genius. Go on!

BASIL

Well, and then, a bit later, came the speech. Richards gave me a sign and I started my strip act. The Minister (*Chuckles*) got red in the face . . . he was just talking about the message of art . . . and when I'd finished, the police arrived. Hugh took some photos of me, I said *"Bon soir"* to the Minister, and they took me away. They wouldn't let me get dressed until we got back to the office.

GEORGIE

Wouldn't let you! (*Laughs*.) Did you want to get dressed?

BASIL

Well . . . I did feel a bit stupid.

ANTOINE

Extremely interesting. Extreeeemely interesting! Have some punch, shark! Drink! Have some of this! (*Passes him a tablet*.)

(BASIL *swallows it*.)

BASIL

(*Kicks the record player. The needle slides*.) Turn off . . . that barrel organ!

(GEORGIE *laughs*.)

That old crock! (*Turns the Tchaikovsky record on to 45 rpm*.) That old box . . . (*Begins to laugh wildly*.)

GEORGIE

The old box . . . of Mr. Cox. (*Laughter*.)

BASIL

Box, cox, fox, pox.

GEORGIE

Mr. Cox . . . (*Laughter.*)

BASIL

(*Laughs. Kicks record cabinet.*) Record box! (*Laughs.*)

ANTOINE

Shark. Control yourself. Shark!

BASIL

(*Kicking.*) I'm a shark . . . hark, hark, hark. (*Plays at being a shark, bites* GEORGIE.) I'm the fastest shark . . . (*Laughs.*)
　(GEORGIE *laughs.*)

ANTOINE

I'm the jellyfish. Hello! Jellyfish!

BASIL

The shark can bark!
　(*All laugh except* FRANK.)

ANTOINE

The jelly with a belly! Shark, eat the jelly with a belly . . . jelly-fishy-wish!

BASIL

Giraffe, don't laugh. (*Laughs.*) Laugh, laugh, laugh!
　(BASIL *rushes round the room, knocking down objects, damaging furniture.*)

FRANK

Be careful! You're not at home!

BASIL

The hedgehog's in the bog! Lock, lock, lock!

ANTOINE

Jellyfish calling shark! Jellyfish calling shark! Jellyfish calling shark! Jelly into the melee!

BASIL

I'm the fast shark! Hark, hark!

GEORGIE

Shark! Hark!

ANTOINE

(*Approaches* BASIL.) Jelly to shark. Jelly to shark. (*Kisses* BASIL *lightly on the cheek.*)
  (BASIL *pushes him away, kicks him.*)

BASIL

Shark to jellyfish! Shark to jellyfish!
  (*Throws* ANTOINE *onto sofa, pushes him with foot.* ANTOINE *giggles.*)
Shark to jellyfish! Shark to jellyfish!
  (ANTOINE *screams and giggles.*)

GEORGIE

(*To* FRANK.) My dear hedgehog . . . why are you sitting alone in your bog?

FRANK

(*Deliberate.*) Ha-ha.
  (BASIL *stands up straight, shaking with laughter.* ANTOINE *and* GEORGIE *are gasping for breath.* GEORGIE *rises, puts her hand over* BASIL'*s mouth, then gives him a long kiss.*)

ANTOINE

Shark swallows giraffe! Shark swallows giraffe! Jellyfish swallows shark. (*Rushes at* BASIL.) Rrrrr!

GEORGIE

The shark can bark!
  (*All laugh except* FRANK. *Pause.*)

BASIL

Well, giraffe, when are you going to sleep with the shark?
(*Glances at* FRANK.)

FRANK

You're all bloody idiots!
(*They breathe heavily, then sit and rest.*)
Smoke a bit of hash and there they are all flat out on the
floor. Well, I must say, you're a lot . . .

BASIL

(*After a pause.*) Georgie girl, I'm going to kill myself.
(*He and* GEORGIE *laugh wildly and look at* FRANK.)

FRANK

(*To* GEORGIE.) Okay . . .

GEORGIE

Okay.

ANTOINE

(*Taking a book from a shelf.*) Now, then. The shark is going to read to us.

FRANK

What is it?

ANTOINE

Fairy tales . . . for children with strong nerves. Come on,
read us a bit, dearest shark.

BASIL

Let the hedgehog read. He is the clever one . . . the sober
one. (*Laughs.*)

ANTOINE

Come on, Frankie-hog.
(*They laugh.*)
Or are you afraid?

FRANK

What are you talking about? Why should I read you fairy tales?

ANTOINE

Oh, come on.

FRANK

Whatever for?

ANTOINE

Because we are all dear little children and we're going to listen attentively . . .

BASIL

Read to us, Uncle Hedgehog!

FRANK

(*Laughs.*) My God, you're all idiots!

GEORGIE

Please, Uncle Hedgehog, read to us!

FRANK

(*Opens the book, smiling.*) What sort of fairy tales are these?

ANTOINE

The best from the world over.

FRANK

All right, just to keep the kids quiet. Which one do you want me to read?

ANTOINE

Where the bookmark is.

FRANK

The Tale of the Little Tree. Right?

ANTOINE

Quite right, hedgehog my dearest. Anyone want some more punch?

(*They shake their heads.*)

FRANK

All right. The Tale of the Little Tree.

(FRANK *tries to sound gay.* GEORGIE *rests her head against* BASIL'*s shoulder.*)

Once upon a time there were a man and his wife. Once upon a time . . . oh . . . (*Reads on.*) They had a nice, big house and a nice, big garden. In the garden there were many flowers, planted in pretty, well-kept beds. Indeed . . . it was hard work to keep it all in good order . . . hhmm. Everyone who passed the garden remarked: "What a wonderful garden." But the greatest pride of the couple and of the garden was a little tree . . .

(FRANK *smiles at the others, who never take their eyes off him.*)

. . . was a little tree. But the little tree gave them much trouble. It did not seem to want to grow. It stood right in the center of the garden, but it did not want to grow into a proper tree. (FRANK *stops.*)

ANTOINE

Carry on, hedgehog!

FRANK

. . . did not want to grow into a proper tree. The little tree had been planted many years ago, but it just would not grow. Nor did it want to strand up . . . eh . . . stand up straight.

(*There is laughter as he misreads the word.*)

The two old people had to protect and sup-prect . . . eh . . . support the tree against wind and weather. At the slightest breath of wind the little tee . . . eh, tree . . . would fall over . . . Someone else read this.

ANTOINE

Read on, hedgehog, read on.

BASIL

Read on, Uncle!

FRANK

(*Hurrying on.*) Often the wife said: "How poorly our little tree looks, how it shivers and shrinks. I hope it will survive the winter." Many times the man lifted it out of the earth and planted it somewhere else, adding fertile soil, but soon afterward it would fall over. The little lee . . . eh . . . the little tree was plitty . . . pretty but not strong enough. It just did not have sufficient strength . . . strength . . . (FRANK *tosses the book onto the floor.*) This is dull.

ANTOINE

But it's terribly exciting!

GEORGIE

You aren't the world's greatest reader!
    (BASIL *presses his face against* GEORGIE'*s dress and laughs.*)

FRANK

(*To* GEORGIE, *rising.*) Are you coming?

GEORGIE

What?

FRANK

I'm going.

GEORGIE

Well, go, then.

FRANK

Come with me.

GEORGIE

Why should I?

FRANK

Because I'm not feeling well.
  (BASIL *laughs*, GEORGIE *giggles*.)

ANTOINE

Have some punch.

FRANK

Come on now, please.

GEORGIE

Are you depressed or something?

FRANK

(*Goes out.*) I'll wait for you outside.
  (GEORGIE *rises and follows him out.*)

GEORGIE

Goodbye, my loves.

ANTOINE

Farewell, giraffe! (*Accompanies her out and returns. To*
BASIL.) Have some punch, shark. Ah well, some people can
take it, others can't. (*Looks at* BASIL.) You can take it all
right. Let me hug you, my precious. Have some punch,
shark.

BASIL

Okay, but I need filling up.
  (ANTOINE *pours him some.*)

ANTOINE

(*Passing him his pipe.*) Have a puff, slickety pig.
  (BASIL *draws, rises.* ANTOINE *looks through* BASIL'*s folder.*)
Great . . . absolutely great. (*Comes closer to* BASIL, *grips
his arm.*) Come with me.

BASIL

Where?

ANTOINE
(*Vaguely.*) Over there.

BASIL
What for?

ANTOINE
Hop into beddie-byes.

BASIL
I'm going.

ANTOINE
Stay here, shark.

BASIL
Why?

ANTOINE
Live with me.

BASIL
What for?

ANTOINE
(*Kissing him on the ear.*) Don't be silly! Have some more punch. (*Pause.*)

BASIL
Are you going to buy this picture?

ANTOINE
Of course I am.

BASIL
How much will you give me for it?

ANTOINE
One hundred pounds.

BASIL
Five hundred.

ANTOINE

All right . . . five hundred, but only because it's you.

BASIL

Give me the money, then.

ANTOINE

(*Goes to get the money.*) All right, if you don't trust me.
Oh well, sharks are distrustful. (*Hands* BASIL £500.)
(BASIL *takes the money.*)

BASIL

Cheerio, jellyfish. (*Starts to go.*)

ANTOINE

(*Clinging to him.*) Stay here, you silly boy.

BASIL

There is the picture. (*Pushes him away.*)

ANTOINE

(*Returns.*) Don't be stupid, slickety pig. Don't be so stupid.
You don't know what I can do for you. Just think!
(BASIL *picks up a glass, breaks off the stem, and ap-
proaches* ANTOINE. ANTOINE *withdraws,* BASIL *follows,*
ANTOINE *stops,* BASIL *comes close to him and presses the
glass against* ANTOINE's *forehead.* ANTOINE *screams.*)

CURTAIN

SCENE SIX

(*The kitchen.* LADY DE MARLIMONT, *smartly dressed,*
GEORGIE, *and* BASIL *are sitting at the table, eating and
drinking.*)

BASIL

(*In a good mood.*) "One hundred," he says. "For a hundred
you won't even get my autograph," I said to him. "Anyway," I said, "I won't give you my autograph," because the
fetishists live in the Congo or on the Amazon in Brazil and
that is where he should get himself dropped by the next
helicopter.

(*All laugh.*)

And what do you think he does, the bloody fool? He gets
out his wallet and offers me five hundred! Ha! Then I see
that he's got at least another two hundred in his wallet . . .
well, wallet, more of a notecase . . . so I say to him, "You
can throw those in as well and then we can talk about art!"
Hehehehe! that's how he laughed.

LADY DE M

You'd better be careful that the tax people don't take it all
away.

BASIL

If they do, even if they take fifty percent, I'll still have
three hundred and fifty for that picture—and it wasn't
particularly good either. That's not too bad, eh?

GEORGIE
Which picture was it?

BASIL
It's called: "Where Is the Artist?" . . . a long row of
hedges and somewhere, I think, is me, a tiny figure among
the hedges. He can spend hours every day trying to spot
me, and his guests can have a go at trying to spot me, and
everybody who goes there can try to spot me. Look a little
closer . . . (*Eating*) . . . look there . . . can you spot
him? There! There he is, the scoundrel who got seven hundred pounds out of me. (*Laughs.*) And best of all, Hugh
Richards, professor of history of art and art critic of a lead-
ing daily, stands there, saying: "Oh well, seven hundred
isn't too much for all those leaves and twigs and sticks and
a headful of straw." Hahaha, did he laugh.

LADY DE M
You're a one! I said to myself straightaway, the first time I
saw him. (*Pointing at* BASIL.) He's going to go a long way.
I didn't know in what direction, but I knew he'd go a long
way. I could have sworn it . . . I could have sworn it . . .
(*She rises, pours champagne, sings: "Tralalala."*)

GEORGIE
Food all right?

BASIL
(*Fascinated by the voluptuous forms of* LADY DE MARLI-
MONT'S *body*.) You're looking exceptionally well today,
darling.

GEORGIE
Go on . . .

BASIL
Not you . . . I mean your mum.

LADY DE M
(*Happily.*) Thank you, kind sir!

GEORGIE
Want some more to drink?

BASIL
I always want more to drink.

LADY DE M
We've run dry. That was the last drop, my darlings.

BASIL
Oh. Well, somebody go and get some. Georgie? Are you going to get some?

GEORGIE
What, me?

LADY DE M
Well, do you expect him to go? It's his big day today.

GEORGIE
I feel sick.

BASIL
Why do you feel sick?

GEORGIE
Don't ask stupid questions.

BASIL
But why?

GEORGIE
Because of the baby, nitwit!

BASIL
Does that make you feel sick?

LADY DE M
He's a sweetie!

BASIL

No one feels sick because of my little fellow. That's a personal insult to me! Off you go.

LADY DE M

Why don't you? The fresh air will do you good.

BASIL

Go on, Georgie, pussy, go and get us something.

GEORGIE

Let's both go.

BASIL

You're not a little girlie any more.

LADY DE M

Off you pop.

BASIL

(*Gives money to* GEORGIE.) There you are, get us three bottles of the same.

GEORGIE

(*Taking money*.) You devil! (*Exit*.)

BASIL

My God, I don't know, women are so complicated—not only women, everybody. Everybody is so complicated, what do you think, Mummy?

LADY DE M

I can't understand any of them. I don't know, we used to have such fun. We always found time to do things and work at the same time. I was on the stage . . . I couldn't afford to stay in bed all day. I would have got bored with it anyway. You're a layabout too, I suppose, but at least you've got some talent, you can afford to lounge about and, looking at it from the practical angle, you're rolling in money, at least for the time being. And that's all that matters, let's be honest. Whoever comes to me, whoever he is, if he hasn't got the lolly, he can lump it. No money, no music!

BASIL

You're so right, Mummy. Frank isn't right for Georgie.

LADY DE M

I think you've already managed to convince her of that.

BASIL

But I'm not right for her either.

LADY DE M

Don't say that. She is just like me, she needs a crook like you. Anyway, she's fallen for you head over heels.

BASIL

That doesn't mean anything. Do you know, Mum, what I need?

LADY DE M

I don't think you need a woman at all . . .

BASIL

Oh yes, I do. I need someone like you.

LADY DE M

For your collection, maybe, but not really.

BASIL

You may be right. But I know I need you terribly just now, Mum.

LADY DE M

(*Ruffles his hair.*) I am forty-three years old, old enough to be your mother.

BASIL

So what? That's no age.

LADY DE M

You're right, you know. I don't know why people go by figures like forty-three.

BASIL

It's all shit. I want you and you want me. What are we waiting for? Eh? (*Goes to hall door.*) What kind of state is he in?

LADY DE M

He's asleep, he's had an injection.

BASIL

(*Putting on a record.*) An injection . . . (*He massages her shoulders, working on them for some time.*)

LADY DE M

You're a monster, Basil.
    (*He spreads the rug on the floor with his feet.*)

BASIL

Come along, madam.

LADY DE M

You're nuts. In any case, Georgie will be back any minute.

BASIL

By the time she gets back we'll be finished, eh? We'll be through by then, the two of us, Mummy.

LADY DE M

Let's do it tomorrow or somewhere else.

BASIL

Here and now! Now and here! (*He pulls her down, she tries to push him away, he hits out at her, pulls off her top.*) Don't make such a fuss.

LADY DE M

Stop it!

BASIL

(*Throws himself on top of her.*) Here and now! (*Raising his voice.*) Here and now!

    (GEORGIE *enters,* BASIL *carries on.*)

GEORGIE

Oh, charming! Very nice! Very nice, indeed. Just you wait!

    (*She runs off.* BASIL *struggles with* LADY DE MARLIMONT.)

LADY DE M

Stop it, she's going to do something to herself.

BASIL

She won't come to any harm.

    (GEORGIE'*s voice is heard.*)

GEORGIE

(*Off.*) Daddy, come and look. Have a look at what she's up to . . . look.

    (*She enters, leading her sick father by the hand and pulling him through the door.*)

GEORGIE

Just look at that.

    (*The old man begins to gasp for breath.* LADY DE MARLIMONT *screams, the old man collapses.*)

LADY DE M

Call the doctor!

GEORGIE

Not me!

    (LADY DE M *slaps her face.*)

LADY DE M

Fool, I could . . .

CURTAIN

SCENE SEVEN

(*The kitchen.* GEORGIE, *visibly pregnant, is cooking. A saucepan is steaming. Pop music from Radio One.* FRANK *enters.*)

FRANK
Hallo there.

GEORGIE
Hallo. All over?

FRANK
I think so. Mind you, I didn't go into the church. I think it's ridiculous that they should have a church wedding.

GEORGIE
Well, Mummy wanted it.

FRANK
Basil didn't.

GEORGIE
Basil said he likes a church wedding because he likes the smell of hash in the church.

FRANK
Bloody idiot. And you're cooking for them?

GEORGIE
Any objections?

FRANK
I really don't understand you.

GEORGIE
Why not?

FRANK
Well.

GEORGIE
Why not!

FRANK
First he gets you pregnant, then he marries your mother—
and there you are cooking away for them. What are you
making?

GEORGIE
Spaghetti.

FRANK
You don't say. As a first course.

GEORGIE
No, main course.

FRANK
Is the wedding lunch somewhere else, then?

GEORGIE
No, here.

FRANK
And you're making spaghetti?

GEORGIE
It's Basil's favorite dish. He eats it three times a week.

FRANK
Don't be ridiculous.

GEORGIE
Did Antoine come?

FRANK

Oh yes, lots of people came. And Hugh took photographs like mad . . . acted like a Hollywood director, he did. Then they took a picture of Mummy holding Basil in her arms like a baby . . . and one where Basil stands with his foot on her and she is lying on the ground, and Antoine went leaping around like a goat and kept calling your mother "llama."

GEORGIE

Try some of this.

FRANK

(*Tasting.*) It's hot . . . not bad.

GEORGIE

Could you lay the table?

FRANK

What me?
    (GEORGIE *kisses him.*)

GEORGIE

You're not cross, are you?

FRANK

Oh, all right. (*Starts to lay the table.*) This place is a mad-house.

GEORGIE

Look, it's quite simple. I'll have the baby and then we can get married.

FRANK

Ha! You don't think I'm going to work my fingers to the bone to keep that brat of Basil's, do you? You're . . .

GEORGIE

No, Mummy is going to keep the baby.

FRANK

(*Laying the table.*) How many will there be?

GEORGIE

Basil, Mummy, Hugh, Antoine, you, and myself—that's six.

FRANK

What a collection. It's not easy to sort out the various relationships.

GEORGIE

You're slowly turning into a good old square.

FRANK

No chance. Where are the happy couple going to sit?

GEORGIE

Wherever you like.

(ANTOINE's *voice is heard outside:* Heave ho!)

BASIL

(*Enters, carrying* LADY DE MARLIMONT.) You're not at all heavy!

(*He puts her down.* LADY DE MARLIMONT *tries to kiss* BASIL. *He is about to turn away, she pulls him back and grabs him wildly.*)

ANTOINE

What a delicious smell! Is that my super special sauce? (*Looks into saucepan, tastes.*) Ouch! It's hot!

LADY DE M

My goodness, children, I am glad all this fuss and bother is over and done with. Food ready, Georgie?

GEORGIE

Yes.

ANTOINE

Our giraffe is an excellent cook. Only it's a bit too hot! (*Giggles, looks at* FRANK.)

BASIL

Hi, Frank, how are you, you old hog! Why didn't you come to church? Believe me, it was tremendous. I'm telling you. It was a dream wedding!

FRANK

Good.

ANTOINE

You know why he didn't go in, don't you? Because the wicked can't stand churches.
(*Everyone smiles.*)

FRANK

Naturally, Antoine, I suppose that's why you were there.
(*Smiles painfully.*)

ANTOINE

Ah well, I'm a saint anyway.

LADY DE M

You've laid the table—that's nice of you, Georgie love.

GEORGIE

I didn't lay the table. Frank did it.

LADY DE M

Frankie, my love, how nice of you.

BASIL

Frankie, the pride of the family! We'll let him eat with us, shall we? What do you say, Frankie?

FRANK

Okay, okay, Basil, we know you're super.

BASIL

Lost your powers of speech, boyo? Tell us, you're not sulking again, are you? People who sulk will not be allowed in here today. Either you laugh or you go! Laugh! Dear friend!

FRANK
(*Artificial laugh.*) Ha-ha-ha.

BASIL
Well, I must say, that was very convincing. (*To* GEORGIE, *embracing her.*) And how is my little giraffe?

GEORGIE
Very well, thanks.

BASIL
(*Caressing her.*) And what is that little scoundrel doing inside there?

GEORGIE
Nothing.

BASIL
Nothing, that's not much.

GEORGIE
Well, you don't expect him to ride around on a bike like you, do you?

BASIL
Why not? What do you think, Mum?

LADY DE M
God, I am looking forward to seeing this little fellow. Just as if he were my own. Well, I suppose he is in a way.

BASIL
(*Sits at the table and rattles his knife and fork.*) Sit down, Mama!

LADY DE M
I must go and change.

BASIL
No, you mustn't go and change. Sit down!

LADY DE M
In a minute.

BASIL
Sit down, I said!
(LADY DE MARLIMONT *sits*.)

GEORGIE
Could you give me a hand, Frank?

FRANK
What with?

GEORGIE
Hold that dish!
(FRANK *holds dish*.)

BASIL
Hurry up, chef. Hahahaha.

FRANK
All in good time.

GEORGIE
Hold it steady, don't wobble.

ANTOINE
He's a wobbler, my little hedgehog is.

FRANK
All right, jellyfish.

BASIL
Throw us some spaghetti, Frank!
(FRANK *takes the dish to the table*.)

GEORGIE

Where is Hugh? (*Doorbell.*) Ah, talk of the devil. Would
you go and open the door, Frank . . .

(FRANK *goes.* BASIL *begins to eat greedily.*)
All right?

BASIL

No need to ask.
(LADY DE MARLIMONT *begins to cry.*)

ANTOINE

Why are you crying, llama?

LADY DE M

It's nothing.

BASIL

My wife is moved. Am I right, Mummy?

LADY DE M

It's all right. I'm better now. It was just the strain.

RICHARDS

God be with you!

BASIL

Welcome, great critic!

RICHARDS

You eating already?

BASIL

Come and join us or it'll all be gone.

RICHARDS

Hang on. Just before I do, I'd like to take a few more photos.
En famille, you might say. The maestro eating spaghetti.
Not bad, eh? (*Looks through camera.*) Just like that, Basil.
Great. Now with your wife. Splendid.

BASIL

Come here, Georgie pussy.

RICHARDS

Smile! Okay.

ANTOINE

(*Begging like a dog.*) Jellyfish would like to be photographed too.

RICHARDS

All right. You join them over there. That's it. Frank, could you move over a bit, or your hand will be in the picture.

FRANK

Are you going to make a movie about the O'Malley family? Rather like the Trapp family . . .

RICHARDS

Talking of the Trapp family—madam, you used to be a singer?

LADY DE M

I was.

RICHARDS

Shouldn't we take one then, where you are singing?

LADY DE M

But why?

ANTOINE

Sing, llama, trill.

BASIL

Of course she can sing, she sings like a blackbird, my little birdie.

LADY DE M

Get away with you. That's all in the past!

BASIL

Listen, my love, you're going to sing now, see, because your Basil likes it, he would like to see your bell-like voice in the photograph.

LADY DE M

Well, I'll pretend I'm singing and you take the picture.

BASIL

You'll sing, or else . . .

ANTOINE

The shark commands, the llama sings. That's nature's law— red in tooth and claw.

RICHARDS

Ready.

LADY DE M

(*Sings.*) "We'll gather lilacs in the spring again . . ."

ANTOINE

Enchanting.

BASIL

That's made me really hungry, the way you open your mouth so wide. Let's eat.
   (*They eat.*)

LADY DE M

If only my dear Charles could have seen this.

BASIL

He'd drop dead again.
   (*Laughter. They eat.*)

RICHARDS

I don't usually like spaghetti, but the way Georgie cooks it, it's super.

ANTOINE

Superbly delicious . . . superbly delicious.
   (*They eat.*)

BASIL

(*After a pause.*) Frank, would you get me the pepper?

FRANK

How do I know where the pepper is?

GEORGIE

Up on the shelf on the left.

FRANK

(*Rises.*) What do you mean, up on the shelf on the left?

GEORGIE

There!

FRANK

I'd call that in the middle to the right.
   (*They eat in silence for some time.*)

ANTOINE

(*Maliciously.*) Hedgehog . . . would you get me some
salt?
   (*All begin to laugh. They laugh more and more.*)

FRANK

You must be joking.

LADY DE M

Frankie, would you get me a glass of water?

FRANK

Shut up, stupid cow! You superannuated tart!

LADY DE M

How dare you?

BASIL

Speak like that to my wife!

FRANK

You shut up, you puppet you, you manipulated puppet.
(*Tosses spaghetti at* BASIL *and* LADY DE MARLIMONT.)

RICHARDS

Don't do that, Frankie.

LADY DE M

Get out of my house, at once! Get out! Basil, throw him
out!

BASIL

Get lost, Frankie! If you soil my beautiful body, you are
no longer my friend!

FRANK

Why should I go? I'm beginning to enjoy myself. It's beginning to look a bit more colorful. I'll go when I feel like
it! I'm not afraid of you waxworks. You can kiss my arse,
you and your dream wedding!
(*He knocks over the table.* BASIL *starts to fight* FRANK.
They fight with their fists, but the fight ends undecided.)

LADY DE M

I'm going to call the police. (*Exit.*)

GEORGIE

Frankie, you're out of your mind!

ANTOINE

The hedgehog is fuming!

RICHARDS

Shame about the spaghetti.
(*Fight ends.*)

FRANK

Bastards! (*To* ANTOINE *and* RICHARDS.) You're great, you are. First you talk big, then you don't have the guts to go through with it. There they are sucking up to him, clinging to him like . . . like limpets.

LADY DE M

(*Enters.*) The police are on their way.

RICHARDS

You don't say. We're going to have some fun. I must put in a new film. (*Puts new film into camera.*)

BASIL

Ladies and gentlemen, make yourselves at home. Pretend nothing has happened. Georgie, puss, get some wine. Nothing has happened . . . because when Frank tries to get something done, nothing ever happens.

ANTOINE

Well, if I might be allowed to comment on all this . . . I think it's all remarkable . . . quite remarkable.

BASIL

(*Pours wine.*) There you are . . . take a glass each . . . cheers!

ANTOINE

Cheers!

RICHARDS

Cheers, maestro!

    (FRANK *lights a cigarette. They drink. Doorbell.* GEORGIE *puts on a record.*)

LADY DE M

(*Goes to the door.*) I'm glad you've come. He's in there, the one with the cigarette.

(*The* POLICEMEN *stop a short distance away from* FRANK.)
Look, Officer, what a mess he has made, that lunatic . . .

1ST POLICE OFFICER
Let's go, young man.

2ND POLICE OFFICER
What are you waiting for, an invitation?

FRANK
(*Snatches a kitchen knife.*) Come here, you bastards, if you
dare . . .

1ST OFFICER
Let's go.

FRANK
Just you try, fascist pig!
   (FRANK *makes as if to attack the* 1ST POLICE OFFICER *with
   his knife. The* 2ND OFFICER *grabs him from behind.* FRANK
   swings round, is thrown off his balance by POLICEMAN'S
   foot and falls, hitting his head on edge of table. LADY DE
   MARLIMONT *and* GEORGIE *scream.*)

BASIL
A hit, a hit, a palpable hit!
   (RICHARDS *takes photographs.*)

CURTAIN

SCENE EIGHT

(*Hospital ward. There are about five beds with patients. Night. There is a strong wind outside. One of the patients groans at regular intervals.* FRANK *tosses and turns in a bed in the foreground. He sits up, turns on his bedside lamp, takes a packet of cigarettes and lights one.*)

1ST PATIENT
(*Sleepy.*) There he goes, stinking the place out again . . . (*Turns over.*)

2ND PATIENT
Do you have to pollute the air? (*Pause.*) You might at least open the window.

FRANK
Okay.
(FRANK *gets out of bed, opens a window, the wind blows in.* FRANK *sits on his bed.* MR. MIDDLETON *wakes up.*)

MIDDLETON
(*Next to* FRANK.) What's happening?

2ND PATIENT
The artist is stinking the place out again.

1ST PATIENT
I don't care what he does as long as he closes the window.

2ND PATIENT
What time is it?

1ST PATIENT
(*Looking at the clock by his bed.*) I make it three.

MIDDLETON
I only make it half past two.

1ST PATIENT
Your clock is always slow.

MIDDLETON
On the contrary, it usually keeps very good time. I only had it repaired the other day.

1ST PATIENT
It's ten to three! The middle of the night.

MIDDLETON
I make it twenty to three. What time do you make it, Mr. Edgar?

2ND PATIENT
I make it exactly half past.

MIDDLETON
Half past what?

2ND PATIENT
Half past twelve. No, that can't be right. It must have stopped.

MIDDLETON
What time do you make it, Mr. Swann?

FRANK
I haven't got a watch.

MIDDLETON
There's a clock above the door, can you see it?

1ST PATIENT
It says a quarter to three.

2ND PATIENT
Two minutes to.

MIDDLETON
I expect that one is correct.

1ST PATIENT
It's only a cheap clock.

MIDDLETON
Cheap clocks often work perfectly.

1ST PATIENT
Would you please close that window? We'll all catch our death. It's snowing outside.

2ND PATIENT
The window will remain open as long as he is smoking. You're not going to die because of a bit of fresh air.

1ST PATIENT
If you like, I'll ring for Nurse and ask her to take you for a walk outside!

2ND PATIENT
Excellent idea. (*He rings for a nurse.*)

MIDDLETON
Gentlemen, we're not going to quarrel, are we? After all, we're all in the same boat.

1ST PATIENT
People in such good health as yourself aren't supposed to be in hospital at all!

MIDDLETON
I think we'll leave the verdict to the consultant and house physician.
    (NURSE PEGGY *enters*.)

PEGGY

You've all got your lights on? Is there anything wrong, duckies? And the window is open! Are you out of your minds!

1ST PATIENT

I'm going to complain to the house physician tomorrow.

PEGGY

(*Closes the window.*) But, Grandpa! (*Kisses his cheek and slaps it playfully.*) There you are, it's already closed, Daddy, and now you're all going to be good boys and go to sleep. And our Frankie here is going to put out his cigarette and turn off the light. (FRANK *puts out cigarette.*) Or else, the boss is going to be cross.

MIDDLETON

Nurse Peggy?

PEGGY

What is it, Mr. Middleton?

MIDDLETON

Would you get me a cup of hot cocoa?

PEGGY

What, now?

MIDDLETON

(*Offering her a chocolate.*) Here you are. It's got a rum filling. If you bring me that cocoa, I'll give you another one.

PEGGY

Very well. But you must keep quiet until all our grumpies have fallen asleep. (*Exit.*)

MIDDLETON

(*To* FRANK—*the others rest and groan.*) Peggy is an angel. Without her I wouldn't be here any more.

FRANK
Why not?

MIDDLETON
I've been a picture of health for the last month. But dear little Peggy puts the curve up on my temperature chart every time I'm due to be discharged.

FRANK
What do you mean?

MIDDLETON
I want to stay! You're a young man, you'll probably think, he's talking nonsense, the old fool! But what am I going to do at home? Specially now during the winter. I've got to heat the place, I've got to cook for myself, I can't afford a housekeeper. I can go to my nephew's to watch the telly, but that's a long way from my place and they don't want me there all the time either. So what shall I do? I've got my food here, there are people I can talk to, or at least have a row with, I can watch the telly, go for a walk . . . what more do you want? The only unpleasant time of the day is the doctor's visit, and having to pretend to be a sick man all the time. But then I've got to save my face in front of the other patients.

FRANK
All on the National Health!

MIDDLETON
That's what it's there for, isn't it? I've never been sick, maybe three or four times in all my life. But I've never been in hospital before. The funniest thing is, the last time I was due to be discharged I took my temperature and guess what? I really did have a temperature, nearly a hundred. A real temperature. I suppose it's psychosomatic.

PEGGY
(*Enters with cocoa.*) Now, drink up quickly and turn off your light! (*She turns off both lamps.*) Nightie-night!

MIDDLETON
Your chocolate!

PEGGY
I'll have it tomorrow, shshsh.

MIDDLETON
Good night, Mr. Swann.

FRANK
Good night.
   (*Pause.*)

MIDDLETON
Excellent cocoa. (*Pause.*) The food is better than in many restaurants. Ah.
   (*He settles down. The wind howls outside,* PATIENTS *groan, one of them dreams aloud.*)
The major is dreaming about the lion again. Every night he attacks him!

VOICE
Bloody Lion! Get away! Get away!

MIDDLETON
It's more amusing than going to the theater. (*Pause.*) It's just like going to the theater . . . after all, normally I never go to the theater.
   (*Pause. Some groans. In the distance, inside the hospital, the sound of laughter and of a transistor radio playing.* BASIL *and* GEORGIE, *the latter very drunk, enter.*)

BASIL
In here! This is the ward of wards!

GEORGIE
But it's all dark!

BASIL
Let there be light!
(FRANK *turns on his light. So does* MIDDLETON.)

FRANK
Are you mad? Don't make so much noise!

BASIL
But, Frankie, my boy! Day is night and night is day.
(*Shouts.*) Wakey, wakey! Good morning! Rise and shine!
(GEORGIE *laughs hysterically.*)
Time for your daily dozen!

FRANK
Shut up!

BASIL
I thought you would be pleased if we came to see you!

FRANK
How on earth did you get in?

GEORGIE
(*Teasing him.*) How on earth did you get in . . . Frankie
pussy . . . Frankie love . . . are you poorly, luvey? Puss
is cross . . . (*Gets into bed with* FRANK.)

FRANK
Go on, get out!

GEORGIE
Get out, he says. But, Frankie my love . . . (*Kisses him.*)
Frankie pussy . . .

MIDDLETON
She's a bit of a passionate one! (*With pleasure.*) A creature
of true breeding!

(*The other* PATIENTS *wake up and watch from their beds with horror and surprise.*)

1ST PATIENT
That's the limit!

2ND PATIENT
Nurse!

BASIL
Gentlemen! Calm yourselves! Have a good look at those two lovebirds! Have a good look—see, gentlemen! Out you get! (*Shakes the bed of the man who groans.*) Out you get, mate! (*Turns up volume of transistor radio. The sick man groans.*) Look how she's gobbling him up, the little whore.

FRANK
Cut it out! Don't be an idiot.
(*She clutches him tightly, he pushes her away.* NURSE PEGGY *enters.*)

PEGGY
Who are you?

BASIL
Who am I? Who are *you?* Little mouse.

PEGGY
What are you doing here?

2ND PATIENT
Get that comedian out of here. (*Rising.*) I'm going to get the house officer.

PEGGY
You're that painter, aren't you, that crazy one . . . Basil O'Malley!

BASIL

Right first time! She knows me, the little mouse.
  (*Hugs her.*)

PEGGY

Let go!

BASIL

Let go, little mo! (*Laughs, lets go of her, gives her a push,
she runs out.*) See you!
  (*Turns volume full up.*)

1ST PATIENT

This is too much!

MIDDLETON

(*To* FRANK.) I don't mind in the least . . . for someone
like myself, in good health, it makes a pleasant change!

BASIL

(*To* MIDDLETON.) Come and swing a leg with me, Great-
granddad! (*Pulls him out of bed and makes as if to dance
with him.*)

FRANK

Get out!
  (*Slaps* GEORGIE's *face.*)

MIDDLETON

My dear sir, I'm afraid I don't know how to dance. I'm sure
your lady-wife here can dance much better!

GEORGIE

Frankie is cross!
  (*Dances wildly with* BASIL. *They dance away from each
other, back to back, making ecstatic movements.* BASIL
stumbles, pulls down the bedclothes, jumps onto FRANK's
bed and dances.

FRANK

(*Leaps up.*) Get off, scram! (*Pushes him off the bed.*) Who do you think you are! Bloody fool!

BASIL

Well said, Frankie. (*Egging him on.*)

FRANK

Bloody country bumpkin, upstart! You primitive ape!
   (BASIL *encourages him.*)

BASIL

Super. Carry on!

FRANK

Infiltrating parasite! Arse-crawling coward! (*Hits out at him.* BASIL *laughs and dances away from him.*)

GEORGIE

Frankie is cross!

BASIL

Frankie is great! He's gigantic!

GEORGIE

He doesn't look gigantic, though. He looks . . . he looks as if he's not at all well. Don't you think? (*Dances.*)

2ND PATIENT

(*Outside.*) Doctor! Doctor! Help!
   (*Two other* PATIENTS, *in nightshirts, appear shyly at the door.*)

GEORGIE

Come and dance with us, Frankie!

1ST PATIENT

(*Opens the window. The wind blows in some snow.*) Police!

GEORGIE

Frankie sweetie, don't you want to build him up? Don't you want to manipulate?

BASIL

Build me up, Frankie! Please, please, do build me up! I'm going to kill myself, Frankie . . . hahaha . . . look . . . (*He winds a sheet round his neck and falls to the ground laughing.*)

GEORGIE

(*To* FRANK.) Why are you pulling such a sour face? Don't you have an urge to build something up? (*Points to her stomach.*) Look, there's something for you to build up. (*Giggles.*) There's something to build up . . . something quite . . . fresh!

(FRANK *hits her, so that she falls to the ground. He goes on hitting at her, hitting her stomach. She screams.*)

BASIL

That's right, Frankie! Let her have it! You're great, Frankie! (*Gales howling through the window, snow, the* PATIENTS *calling, running about, utter chaos.* DOCTOR *and* NURSES *enter.*)

DOCTOR

What's going on? (*To the* NURSES.) Help her up. (*They help* GEORGIE *up.*)

GEORGIE

(*Cries out with pain.*) Ououou. (GEORGIE *is led outside.*)

DOCTOR

Who the hell are you? What are you doing in here?

BASIL

I shall feel insulted if you don't recognize me, sir!

DOCTOR

You must be out of your mind if you think you can behave like a hooligan in this hospital.

BASIL

My name is Basil O'Malley, if that means anything to you.

DOCTOR

O'Malley. I don't care what your name is. See that you leave here at once. (*To* PATIENTS.) Quick-march back into your beds. What do you think you are in here for? You too, Mr. Middleton. Or else you'll run a temperature again!

MIDDLETON

I feel a bit feverish already.

DOCTOR

And you too, Mr. Swann. I haven't experienced anything like this in my thirty years as a doctor!

2ND PATIENT

You see, Doctor, it was like this . . .

DOCTOR

Go to sleep, I don't want to hear another word.
    (*A* NURSE *enters hurriedly.*)

NURSE

Geoffrey!

DOCTOR

What is it?

NURSE

She has lost the baby.
    (*The* DOCTOR *rushes out.*)

BASIL

(*To* FRANK.) Cheerio then, I'm off home. You coming?

FRANK

What for?

BASIL

I expect Hugh will be there, and my wife . . . Antoine
. . . I don't suppose we shall get to bed before eight in the
morning.

FRANK

I might come round later . . . when things have calmed
down a bit.

BASIL

Yes, do come, dear old pal. Everything's back to normal
now. Like the good old days.

FRANK

Well . . . I suppose so. (*Lights a cigarette.*)

BASIL

See you. (*Exit.*)

1ST PATIENT

Now he's smoking again.

CURTAIN

SCENE NINE

(BASIL's *studio. Comfortably and expensively furnished, spacious.* BASIL's *wife asleep in an armchair. Next to her is a bottle of whisky, half empty. She snores loudly. Half a minute later* BASIL *enters.* PEGGY, *the nurse, follows hesitantly.*)

BASIL
(*To* PEGGY.) Asleep! (*He creeps up to her, holds her nose. She lets out a distorted howl.*) The old sow's fighting for oxygen.

LADY DE M
Stop it, Basil.

BASIL
I'm extremely put out to find you . . . to find you in this state.

LADY DE M
Well, if you don't come home.

BASIL
(*To* PEGGY.) Sit down, beautiful! (*Offers her a chair.*)

LADY DE M
What have you got with you this time? Who's this teen-ager?

BASIL
This isn't a teen-ager, duckie, this is a lady! A working woman! She works day and night!

LADY DE M

I can well imagine!

BASIL

Not the way you think, in your filthy bourgeois mind. She is a respectable lady. And she is going to stay the night with us. Eh, Peggy? And I shall make myself personally responsible to make sure that nothing indecent happens to her. That's why, in these exceptional circumstances, she is going to sleep in my bed!

LADY DE M

Don't talk rubbish. You're mad! For three weeks now we've had these respectable ladies . . .

BASIL

Shut up! (*Grips her, stares at her.*) Will you shut your trap. You know what happens, Mum, if you don't shut up. (*Walks round the studio.*) Nothing but idle gossip.

LADY DE M

I'm leaving.

BASIL

That's just what you're waiting for, isn't it, you old sow? But you're going to stay here, because Richards will be here soon and he's quite keen on you, ducks. We'll all change round. Okay?

LADY DE M

That's what you think! Once and never again. You can keep your learned critic.

BASIL

Mummy, my love, don't you dare, I'm telling you. Richards is a friend of mine, don't you dare despise my friends.

PEGGY

I think I'd better go.

LADY DE M

Yes, you'd better.

BASIL

You're going to stay, beautiful! No one's going. No one's leaving, everyone's going to stay. We're going to get on very well together! You two are going to be the best of friends. Show Peggy the bed, love, and then she can go to bed whenever she's tired.

PEGGY

I'm not a bit tired.

BASIL

That's fine, then. But you will be, very tired, believe me. (*Looks around.*) What a mess. You, at forty-four, ought to have some sense of order! Why do you think I married you! An artist needs someone to keep things tidy for him. So: Tidy up! Tidy up! That's your job! Show your good family background! Ha! Old and messy too! What do you think of that, Peggy my gorgeous?

(*Kisses* PEGGY. LADY DE MARLIMONT *begins to cry.*)

PEGGY

Look, she's crying.

BASIL

Crying? Out of the question, chick! (*Moves to her.*) Come on, no crying now, understand? (*Sings.*) "Keep smiling through . . ." (*She cries louder.*) Basil is with you and he loves you very much. "Keep smiling through . . ."

LADY DE M

(*To* PEGGY.) If you only knew what he gets up to every night. And I'm supposed to be . . . (*Cries.*) . . . I'm supposed to be his servant. And I do it for him, silly ass that I am!

PEGGY
But why are you doing it?

LADY DE M
You don't know what it's like when you love someone, and I do love that rascal! I love him so much, even though he's always hitting me. Why are you so cruel to me all the time? I do everything you ask of me.

BASIL
That'll do now. Go and wash your face. Richards will be here any minute and he doesn't like those watery crocodile eyes! He wants to see those two bright-blue little sparklers in your face. Go and wash, put on some makeup, and then tidy up a bit. Then we'll all love you. Okay? Say yes, honey-bunch, say yes.

LADY DE M
Yes.

BASIL
You're a darling sweetie pie. (*She goes out. To* PEGGY.) You look quite worn out, beautiful. You mustn't let the moods of my beloved spouse get you down!

PEGGY
Have you got a record player?

BASIL
Silly question. There it is. Wait a minute.

PEGGY
Got a Beatles record?

BASIL
Not only but also! Not only but also!
(*Puts on "Light My Fire."*)

PEGGY
That's fabulous.
(*They dance. Doorbell.*)

BASIL
Go and open, honeybunch!

LADY DE M
(*Off.*) I'm just putting on some makeup! You go!

BASIL
(*Calls.*) Step inside!

RICHARDS
(*Enters.*) And how is our great maestro this evening?

BASIL
I welcome you with body and soul! Help yourself to whisky.

RICHARDS
Just what I need. I've been working myself to death over some idiotic article.

BASIL
This is Peggy. Come and join us, Hugh. We've just met at the hospital.
(RICHARDS *joins in dance.*)

RICHARDS
Been to the hospital? To see Frank?

BASIL
Yes. It was most enjoyable. A most enjoyable evening. Georgie got rid of her baby at the same time. Yeah . . . all very successful.

RICHARDS
How come?

BASIL

Well, Frank pulled a few punches and the baby didn't like it.

RICHARDS

You don't say.

BASIL

Oh yes . . . Frank is feeling a lot better now. He may be coming round later.

RICHARDS

I'd be surprised if he dared enter the lion's den.

BASIL

It's a bit of a drag without Frankie. (*Pulling* PEGGY *closer*.) Peggy, my sweet!

RICHARDS

Where's your lovely wife?

BASIL

She's dressing up for you, Hugh. You'll have to watch it tonight, she's out to get you . . .

RICHARDS

I've got lots of energy to use up after writing that article.

(LADY DE MARLIMONT *appears in the door, all dolled up*.)

LADY DE M

May I join in?

PEGGY

That's the end of the record.

BASIL

You come in and the record stops.

LADY DE M

Don't tell me it's my fault that the record is finished.

(*She puts record on again, dances up to* RICHARDS, *they*

dance in a clinch. ANTOINE *enters with a bottle of whisky in his hand.*)

ANTOINE

Who cometh walking upon the wind
And riding high upon the storm
It is Antoine—the wiggly worm.
(*Laughs piercingly.*) Let me kiss you, beloved!

BASIL

Hello there, old ass.

ANTOINE

Hello, hello, hello . . . a new face! Ah, that's without doubt a young okapi. That's something very special indeed.

BASIL

(*To* PEGGY.) If you think he's soft in the head, you're mistaken. The gentleman is perfectly normal.

PEGGY

I'm not so sure.

ANTOINE

Okapis are never quite sure, remember that. Even the Good Lord was not quite sure what sort of an animal to create . . . even the Good Lord had His doubts on that score!

BASIL

Where have you been all this time?

ANTOINE

In my own little room. Yes, I've been sitting in my own little room, discussing the theory of mysticism with Mama . . .
    (PEGGY *giggles.*)
There's nothing to laugh about, okapi. Things are somewhat complex . . . they couldn't get any complex-er! Cheers, my lord!

BASIL

Cheers, you old philosophizer!
  (FRANK *enters in dressing gown and pajamas.*)

FRANK

Hello, everyone!
  (*He seems gayer and more cheerful.*)

BASIL

Frank, my dearest! Look who's here, everybody!

RICHARDS

Been to a pajama party?

PEGGY

If the house surgeon gets to know about this! You're supposed to stay in bed another week.

BASIL

He can stay in bed wherever he is! Have a drink, mate!

FRANK

Thanks. You know, I'm so glad to be out of that bloody
hospital.

PEGGY

How's your lady friend?

FRANK

They say she's better.

BASIL

Still cross that we came?

FRANK

No, but you know, being in hospital and all that, Georgie
really got on my nerves with all that fuss.

BASIL

She was a bit on the fatty side. Now then, everybody. We're
all together again, one large family!

FRANK

What I find is amazing is that I keep coming back to you.

BASIL

You're our yo-yo, or whatever it's called.

FRANK

That's what I feel like. But what can I do? . . . a game's a game. And without a game to play I can't exist. Now I feel all right again for the first time in ages.

BASIL

I suppose it was that liberating blow.

FRANK

Maybe you're right.

ANTOINE

I'm telling you, hedgehog: it's important to be with it, not just on the edge of things . . . and the readiness is all, as the great bard so perceptively remarked.

(FRANK *puts on a rock record, laughs, starts to dance.*)

BASIL

(*Laughs.*) Rock! Rock!

(*He starts to rock wildly with* PEGGY. ANTOINE *dances by himself, making boxerlike movements.* RICHARDS *dances with* LADY DE MARLIMONT, *quickly reaching a euphoric state.*)

All change!

(*He pushes* PEGGY *toward* FRANK *and dances with* ANTOINE.)

All change!

(*He dances with his wife,* FRANK *with* RICHARDS, *and* PEGGY *with* ANTOINE.)

All change!

(BASIL *takes off his top, takes* PEGGY's *sweater, they exchange clothes.*)

All change!

(*The others do the same.*)

All change. Rock!

(*Dancing continues with varying changes—hectic dressing and undressing and calls of "All change!" At the end they are exhausted and make for the whisky bottles.*)

LADY DE M

Phhooo, I'm hot! I must have a drink.

PEGGY

Let's put it on again!

FRANK

I'm going to sit this one out.

BASIL

Have a drink.

FRANK

Fill it up, then. (*Drinks.*)

RICHARDS

No more rock for me . . . or else I'll go home and finish writing my article.

FRANK

What are you writing about?

RICHARDS

Basil.

FRANK

What about Basil?

RICHARDS

A comparison with Stubbs.

BASIL

I'm a great admirer of Stubbs. Listen, I'll tell you what we're

going to do now! We're going to play the game of total
change!

RICHARDS
You can count me out.

LADY DE M
Me too.

BASIL
We'll see. You don't have to dance. This is how it goes.
(*Makes a movement as if to throw away his own body.*)
Everybody throws away his own stinking body and takes
someone else's stinking body.

RICHARDS
Okay. My clean body won't be able to take part.

BASIL
Antoine is going to be Mum . . .

LADY DE M
Stop calling me Mum . . .

BASIL
Antoine is my wife, and my wife is Antoine. Hugh is . . .
let's say . . . the late Air Vice-Marshal, Peggy is someone
she knows . . .

PEGGY
Mr. Middleton!

BASIL
Frank is me and I am Frank!

LADY DE M
And what's all that supposed to mean?

BASIL
Just a game to while away the time, Mummy dear.

ANTOINE
Splendid. I am the llama!

BASIL
That's it.

ANTOINE
"We'll gather lilacs in the spring again . . ."

FRANK
(*Laughs.*) That's great. Basil, you're really getting to be
something.

BASIL
Basil is a genius!

RICHARDS
What about me? What am I supposed to do? Call the Pope?

BASIL
Certainly.

RICHARDS
The Pope . . . the Pope . . . Whore! Tart! . . . Who is
that man . . . who is that man?
(*Everyone is amused.*)

BASIL
And you are Antoine, Mama.

LADY DE M
Go on.

ANTOINE
You are my former body, llama!

LADY DE M
What, do you want me to call him llama?

BASIL
You've got it, pussycat!

PEGGY

May I try Mr. Middleton?

BASIL

But of course, beautiful! (*Puts on slow record.*) Right. Take your seats. Fasten your seat belts! We're off.
(*They sit in a circle, drink, and smoke.*)

BASIL

All change! I should like to point out that this is my own invention, copyright reserved.

FRANK

A kind of parlor game.

BASIL

Nonsense. Parlor game—I wouldn't want to take part in anything as obscene, would I, Mum? Play forfeits with car keys or strip poker or other such childish things . . . oh no. The All Change game is different . . . it's a serious game and has nothing to do with sex or the erotic.

ANTOINE

It's quite a remarkable game.

BASIL

The important thing is to look each other in the eye.

FRANK

Stare each other out.

BASIL

If you like, okay. (*To* FRANK, *speaking as* FRANK.) You know, you ought to read a bit, Basil . . . it's all very well to be naïve, but . . . you know . . . you must become more relaxed. Read *Molloy*, for instance, or Joyce. (*They all look at* FRANK.)

FRANK

That's another of those tricks like the one with the fairy tale.

BASIL

A first warning, Frank.

ANTOINE

What was that about a fairy tale? I wasn't there, slickety pig. (*Looks at* FRANK.)

BASIL

(*To* ANTOINE.) You know, we were reading fairy tales, Mrs. O'Malley, and I . . . I had to read aloud. But I couldn't read so well . . .

RICHARDS

The Pope . . . the Pope! (*Rises, walks about. Points to* FRANK.) Who is that? Who is that? (*To* ANTOINE.) You whore, you . . . Brothel madam! She's fucking, the old sow!

ANTOINE

That's not true, Charles . . . it's not true!

LADY DE M

I don't like you making jokes about Charles.

BASIL

(*To her.*) Antoine! Don't pinch me. Don't pinch me, jelly-fish! Listen, Antoine, how about helping a bit with building up Basil . . . help him along a bit . . . you know, build him up . . . and then drop him.

LADY DE M

(*Laughs.*) Splendid! Absolutely diabolical, Basil!

BASIL

Not Basil, I am Frank.

LADY DE M

Hedgehog . . .
    (RICHARDS *walks about talking to himself.*)

PEGGY

Oh, I've got a temperature . . . I feel so ill . . .

ANTOINE

(*Moves to* FRANK.) Basil, my love, come into the room next door. It's your marital duty, Basil.

BASIL

(*To* ANTOINE.) No, pussycat, he's got to be made to loosen up a bit first, you know, pussycat . . . listen to jazz, read Beckett . . .
(*They all look at* FRANK.)

FRANK

(*To himself.*) Okay, I'll join in.

LADY DE M

Slickety pig is going to join in.

FRANK

(*To* BASIL.) You know, Frank, all your wisdom is a lot of shit. If you wanted to build me up, you've slipped up, boyo. I've heard it all from Georgie or whatever her name is. I slept with her in the kitchen the other night.

BASIL

Okay, okay . . . that's great. Couldn't be better. It's fantastic, that fits perfectly into my plan.

ANTOINE

(*To* FRANK.) Basil darling, tell us the story about the reception.

FRANK

(*Draining a glass of whisky.*) Go on, how many more times am I supposed to tell?

ANTOINE

Tell us . . .

FRANK

Well, they were all lining up, as if they were queueing outside the breadshop, and pressed the Minister's clammy
hand . . . so I said: "*Bon soir, monsieur.*" The Minister
replies: "*Bon soir, monsieur.*" So I say: "Oh, I've made a
mistake . . . I am British . . ."

(*They laugh.*)

LADY DE M

Great, slickety pig!

BASIL

Tell us how you stripped!

FRANK

Well, I just took my clothes off . . . you see . . . the
Minister was talking about the eternal redeeming message
of art . . . and he got more and more red in the face . . .

ANTOINE

Like you, my love! (*Kisses* FRANK.)

LADY DE M

(*To* BASIL.) Hedgehog dearest, read us a fairy tale!

BASIL

Oh, no, I don't know. It's a bit childish. I don't know . . .
I don't know.

ANTOINE

(*Taking a book from the shelf, to* BASIL.) Read, Frank!

FRANK

Looks a pretty boring story.

BASIL

(*Fending off.*) No . . . I don't want to read now. I sense
trouble.

ANTOINE
Go on, read!

LADY DE M
Diabolical!

RICHARDS
The Pope . . . (*To* ANTOINE.) Whore, tart, etc.

BASIL
All right, then. ("*Reading.*") The Tale of the Little Tree
. . . Shall I go on?

ANTOINE
Read on!

BASIL
Once upon a time, there lived a man and his wife and they
had a little tree. (*Breathing heavily.*) . . . They had a little tree . . . (FRANK *laughs hysterically*) . . . in a beautiful garden. But the tee . . . eh, eh . . . the tree didn't
want to stay . . . eh, eh . . . stand against the wind and
the weather. It gave them much trouble . . . they replanted
it. But it would not go . . . eh, eh . . . grow that tee . . .
eh . . . No, I can't read now. (*Rises.*) I must go . . . I
feel sick.
(FRANK *laughs hysterically.*)

ANTOINE
(*To* RICHARDS.) I'm good, Charles . . .

RICHARDS
No! You're lyyying! Whore! You're deceiving me with
the Pope!
(*They laugh.*)

ANTOINE
No, with Basil.

RICHARDS

(*Pretending to collapse.*) Eeeeehhhh! (*Drops to the ground.*)

    (GEORGIE *enters, she is still weak, goes straight up to* BASIL, *falls into his arms and cries.*)

LADY DE M

Georgie, darling!

FRANK

(*Jumps to his feet.*) There she goes again! Crying again! My God! Christ, how mixed up you are! I'm telling you, believe me! I'm telling you. (*Goes to record player, puts on rock number.*) Up you get, you lame ducks, we're going to dance! All change! (*To* ANTOINE.) Come here, pussycat! Come to me! Kiss my toes!

    (ANTOINE *kisses his feet.*)

ANTOINE

But don't hit me, Basil my love!

RICHARDS

(*Rising.*) The Pope . . . (*To* ANTOINE.) You whore . . . you common slut!

FRANK

Let's dance, everybody.

    (*Pulls* PEGGY *toward him.*)

    (*During this scene* BASIL *and* GEORGIE *sit in an armchair. They are tenderly in love, which, in turn, causes an artificial euphoria. The others rock and scream.*)

LADY DE M

Slickety pig. Come dance with me. Llama! Llama!

ANTOINE

"We'll gather lilacs in the spring again" . . . Rock, rock. All change!

RICHARDS

The Pope . . . Pope—rock . . . Whore—rock . . .

FRANK

(*To* PEGGY.) Rock, midget, rock . . . or are your bones
dried up to dust!

PEGGY

Not so tight.

FRANK

Not so tight? You're going to get to know me, little mouse.
(*Shakes her brutally.*)

PEGGY

Stop it! (*Tries to break away.*)

FRANK

(*Pulls her back.*) You stay here with your Uncle Basil!

PEGGY

Ouch!

FRANK

(*Falls upon her and to the ground.*) Here and now! Here
and now! (*The others dance around them.*) Here and now!

ALL

Here and now!

PEGGY

Let me go! Basil! Basil!
(BASIL *kisses* GEORGIE.)
(RICHARDS *falls to the ground crying:* "*The Pope.*")
(ANTOINE *clings to* FRANK, *calling:* "*Basil, my love.*")
(PEGGY *scratches* FRANK.)

FRANK

Ouch!
(PEGGY *frees herself, picks up her coat, and runs out of*

the room. The record is finished. They breathe heavily and relax. FRANK *lights a cigarette and goes out of the room.*)

RICHARDS
Let's open the window, it's too hot in here.

LADY DE M
Don't bother, Hugh, I'll do it.
(*She opens a large window. Rain and sleet are falling, and gales are blowing outside.* RICHARDS, ANTOINE, *and* LADY DE MARLIMONT *walk about breathing heavily, wiping their foreheads and drinking.* BASIL *comforts* GEORGIE.)

BASIL
It's all right, my little pussy, my little . . . it's all right.

GEORGIE
Can I have something to drink?

BASIL
There you are.

GEORGIE
No, not alcohol . . . wait a minute, I'll get some water.

BASIL
I'll get you some . . .

GEORGIE
No, it's all right.
(*She goes out. They sit and stare.*)

BASIL
An enjoyable evening, don't you think?

RICHARDS
Not bad.
(LADY DE MARLIMONT *falls asleep in her chair.*)

ANTOINE

A diabolical evening. (*Goes to the window, calls into the wind.*)
Blow, blow, thou winter wind—
Shall I compare thee to a summer's day . . .
 (RICHARDS *turns off center light.*)

BASIL

Fresh air is the best drink . . .
 (ANTOINE *plays an excerpt from the Storm Scene in* King Lear, *then sits.*)
 (LADY DE MARLIMONT *begins to snore. For some time only snoring is heard. Then a short cry from* GEORGIE. *She appears in the door.*)

GEORGIE

It's Frank!

BASIL

What's the matter?
 (GEORGIE *indicates hanging.*)

BASIL

(*Cries.*) He's hanged himself?

GEORGIE

In the loo.
 (*For some time only snoring is heard, then* BASIL *goes up to* LADY DE MARLIMONT *and holds her nose. She wakes up gasping for breath.*)

MAGIC AFTERNOON

Translated and adapted by
Herb Greer

Characters

BRIGIT
MONIKA
CHARLEY
JOE

(BRIGIT, MONIKA, CHARLEY, *and* JOE *are out of their teens but trapped in a kind of identity vacuum, neither adolescents nor adults, uncommitted to anything. Their behavior projects a kind of constant put-on which veils their desperate anomie, as well as an empty anxiety at having nothing worthwhile to be and nothing interesting to do. These are potential "true believers" who have never found a leader and who have neither the vitality nor the courage, nor even—any more—the biological impulse to strike out into an existence as mature human beings.*)

(*Scene: A sloppy bed-sitter in* CHARLEY's *bachelor flat. The big unmade double bed in the center is scattered with the detritus of a bored and pointless existence, which litters the whole room: newspapers, "serious" paperbacks —of both classics and modern writers—various underground publications, porn magazines, tit magazines, especially* Playboy, *plus numerous LPs—some in their sleeves, some not—the latest in pop plus standards like Simon and Garfunkel, Dylan, Wilson Pickett, John Coltrane, Roland Kirk, Shostakovich, Beethoven, Vivaldi, Bach, etc. Among the records and reading material is strewn a mess of dirty dishes, empty booze and milk bottles, etc. There is a TV set, a wardrobe, a stool or two, mats on the floor, chairs, a gramophone, a small table with a dusty typewriter on it, lamps, a large window at the back with venetian blinds up, psychedelic-patterned drapes, and on the obviously hand-painted walls are posters, pictures of Mao, Che, etc., and perhaps a couple of C. Logue's poster poems. There are exits to the kitchen, the bathroom, and the hall. Outside, a beautiful summer afternoon with sun pouring in through the window, birds singing.* CHARLEY *and* BRIGIT *are maneuvering in front of a large mirror.* BRIGIT *is examining the effect of no bra and a thin T shirt,* CHARLEY *trying to comb his hair. They are sharing a cigarette.)*

BRIGIT
(Taking the cigarette from him.) Why don't *you* light one?

CHARLEY
(Flops on the bed, looking for the pack.) What did you do with 'em?

BRIGIT
(Suddenly curious, lifts up the T shirt to expose her breasts, peering into the mirror.) Hey, did you see this?

CHARLEY
(Rooting in her handbag.) Uh huh.

BRIGIT
Charley, look!

CHARLEY
(Groping in her Levi's hip pockets.) Come on, where did you put 'em?

BRIGIT
Charley, one is bigger than the other!

CHARLEY
(Absently, looking for the cigarettes among the trash.) I know. It crosses over just a little. The left one.

BRIGIT
(Peering into the mirror.) The left one?

CHARLEY

What did you do with the fags?

BRIGIT

What do you mean, crosses over?

CHARLEY

When you kiss me. Like this. (*Crosses his eyes.*)

BRIGIT

Not my eyes, my tits! You see? One is bigger than the other!

CHARLEY

(*Finds the pack under the bed: empty.*) Shit! You got the last one.

BRIGIT

(*Sighs, finds her jacket, takes a pack out of the pocket, throws it to* CHARLEY.) What time is it?

CHARLEY

No idea. Two?

BRIGIT

What are we doing tonight? (*Lights another cigarette.*)

CHARLEY

No idea.

BRIGIT

It must be about three . . . I left at eleven . . . about four hours . . .

CHARLEY

(*Picks up the phone, dials "time."*) Two-thirty . . . (*Wanders around the room.*) Peep . . . peep . . . peep . . . at the third stroke it will be two-thirty and ten seconds . . . peep peep peep . . . (*Looking for a match to light his cigarette.*) Three-thirty . . . peep . . . four-thirty

. . . peep . . . five-thirty . . . peep . . . (*Falsetto chant, imitating the operator.*) The sands of time remorselessly run o-on . . . peep . . . and o-on . . . peep peep . . . and o-on . . . peep peep peep . . .

BRIGIT
(*Bored, has heard this before.*) So there's nothing we can do tonight?

CHARLEY
I don't know. What do you want to do?

BRIGIT
I don't know. What do you want to do?

CHARLEY
Go for a walk?

BRIGIT
In this heat?

CHARLEY
Fuckall else we *can* do.

BRIGIT
What you mean is, you're broke again.

CHARLEY
Can't you get something from your mum?

BRIGIT
(*She has heard this before.*) Six dollars, maybe seven . . . that won't take us very far.

CHARLEY
(*Picks up a gin bottle and drinks instead of lighting his cigarette.*) Well, seven dollars . . .

BRIGIT
(*Reaches for the bottle, but he keeps it.*) Can't you get some bread?

CHARLEY
Larry owes me a twenty . . . but he's out of town.

BRIGIT
(*Still wants the bottle.*) *Come* on, love . . . (*Takes the bottle.*)

CHARLEY
Go swimming?

BRIGIT
I don't have my bikini.

CHARLEY
Who needs that old thing? (*Leers unconvincingly.*)

BRIGIT
We could go to Eddie's. He's dying to show me his boat.

CHARLEY
He's dying to show you his cock. Anyway, the car's not ready yet.

BRIGIT
You mean you haven't paid them yet.

CHARLEY
Darling, I spent it all on you! (*Pause.*) Stupid . . .
(*Long pause.*)

BRIGIT
Stupider and stupider.

CHARLEY
Right.

BRIGIT
According to you.

CHARLEY
According to you. (*Shakes himself all over.*) Aaaahhh!

BRIGIT

(*Sighs.*) Is there anything else to eat?

CHARLEY

Uuh . . . some rye bread, I think.

BRIGIT

Salami? No.

CHARLEY

(*Sighs.*) Ah . . . there must be something out there . . .

BRIGIT

(*Goes out to the kitchen, leaves the door open.*) There's something . . . it looks like cheese or something . . . can I take that?

CHARLEY

Yeah . . . don't take it all. (*Picks up a newspaper.*)

BRIGIT

(*Off.*) It tastes funny. How long have you had it?

CHARLEY

I don't know . . . couple of weeks, I guess.

BRIGIT

(*Spitting sounds.*) You bastard!
(*Comes in, washing out her mouth with gulps of Pepsi-Cola, sprays it at him.* CHARLEY *protects himself with the newspaper.*)
Whooo—the gin made me thirsty.

CHARLEY

(*Peeping over the edge of the newspaper.*) Fizz . . . fizz . . . gin fizz.

BRIGIT

(*Empties the bottle, turns it upside down.*) Peace. (*Settles*

behind CHARLEY, *runs her fingers through his hair.*) Hey
. . . you . . . (*Pause.*)

CHARLEY
Hmmmmmm?

BRIGIT
Movies?

CHARLEY
Nothing.

BRIGIT
(*Takes the paper, points.*) What about that one?

CHARLEY
I saw the preview. Catherine Deneuve and her flaccid
thighs. Nothing.

BRIGIT
What about this one? . . .

CHARLEY
Not to be missed . . . yech.

BRIGIT
I wouldn't mind seeing something . . . serious.

CHARLEY
Nobody's stopping you.

BRIGIT
But there *isn't* anything else!

CHARLEY
If I did go . . . ahhh . . . (*Takes the paper.*) *Deep
Throat* . . .

BRIGIT
If you go to that, you'll go by yourself.

CHARLEY

(*Languidly gives the paper back to her.*) Have another look.
All I see is nothing.

BRIGIT

Gone with the Wind?

CHARLEY

Jesus, not again! Isn't there anything really . . . *really*
shitty?

BRIGIT

At the Rialto . . . *The Swedish Au Pair* . . .

CHARLEY

Heeyyy, right! Something really titty! Let's go!

BRIGIT

It's so *far* to the Rialto . . .

CHARLEY

(*Childish lisp.*) Can't I go to see the nasty mooovie?

BRIGIT

What about the theater?

CHARLEY

Whaaat? You want to go . . . to . . . (*Affected tone.*)
the *theyuhtuh*?

BRIGIT

Tomorrow there's *King Lear* again.

CHARLEY

(*Bored.*) Uh huh. And day after tomorrow?

BRIGIT

(*Leafing through the paper.*) It doesn't say . . . maybe it's
in the week's events.

CHARLEY

(*Gets into bed.*) I'm going to sleep.

BRIGIT

(*Dropping the paper.*) You have any more jam . . . hey?

CHARLEY

Oh, have a look . . . but I'm not going down now . . . not for that.

BRIGIT

(*Kneels on the bed, tickles him.*) Pleeease . . . pretty please . . . nice jam . . . pretty please . . . with *sugar* on it . . . nice jam? Nice jam?

CHARLEY

(*Gives up, gets out of bed.*) What kind?

BRIGIT

Peach . . . or black grape!

CHARLEY

All they've got is black cherry and sour plum.

BRIGIT

Really nothing else?

CHARLEY

You've scoffed all the others.

BRIGIT

Then . . . sour plum. And see if there isn't something else. Black grape . . .

CHARLEY

(*Wearily.*) Okay . . . (*He goes out.*)

BRIGIT

(*Puts on a record: "Penny Lane." Looks at her breasts in the mirror again, lifts her T shirt. Then has a thought and runs to the window.*) Charley! Charley!

CHARLEY

(*Off.*) What?

BRIGIT

When was thalidomide invented?

CHARLEY

(*Off.*) Whaat?

BRIGIT

Never mind. Hurry up!
(*Goes back to the mirror, lifts the T shirt, weighs each breast in a hand.*)
God! One is heavier, too!
(*Begins to strike poses à la* Playboy, *unzips the fly of her Levi's, the poses become more and more ridiculous, she becomes rather excited with herself. She begins to make faces to go with the poses, sticking her lips out, licking them, etc. One of the poses proves difficult. She gets a slight crick in her back and tries again.*)
Damn . . . how do they do it?
(*She tries, but it's not quite right. She tries something else and that's better. Tries uncovering one breast and then the other, then both, then pulling down the T shirt tightly over her breasts. She reaches out and strokes the mirror lustfully.*)
De-licious!
(*Turns her back to the mirror, pulls down the Levi's to expose her bum. She spies a spot.*)
Oh, hell!
(*She tries to squeeze the spot, but the location is awkward.*)
Tch . . . shit!
(*She manages at last, examines the result on her fingernail, and flicks it away. Then she looks longingly at herself over her shoulder and blows a kiss at the mirror. The*

telephone rings. Pulls Levi's up and T shirt down and goes to the window.)
Charley! Shall I answer the phone?

CHARLEY
(*Off.*) Leave it!

BRIGIT
Why not?
(*Heavy steps on the stairs.*)

CHARLEY
(*Entering with the jam.*) Let it ring.

BRIGIT
But why?

CHARLEY
Oh, Jesus, answer it, then . . .

BRIGIT
(*Picks up the phone.*) Hello? Hi! Uh huh . . . just fine
. . . (*Hands the receiver to* CHARLEY.)

CHARLEY
Yeah . . . hey, man! Yeah. Fuckall, man. Nah, fuckall. Uh
huh. Uh huh. Yeah. Just sitting here. Yeah. Ma*ma* is away.
Yeah. When? Wild. Tonight. Tonight, man. Nothing so
far. We thought about the mooovies. Only thing is . . .
right. No bread. Right. Hey! Yeah, man, I don't care. Uh
huh. We're almost out of booze. Gin. If you . . . yeah
. . . uh huh . . . uh huh . . . uh huh . . . right. Right.
Yeah. Yeah . . . yeah. Yeah. Naturally! Maybe if . . .
okay . . . okay . . . yeah . . . yeah . . . who, you?
How do you mean? Yeah . . . always the same, yeah . . .
hey! (*Laughs.*) Right. Uh-uh. Uh-uh . . . you come here
. . . sure . . . yeah . . . uh huh . . . yeah . . . yeah

. . . yeah . . . yeah . . . yeah . . . yeah . . . ee*yeah!*
Stay cool.
(*Hangs up.*)

BRIGIT
Is he coming?

CHARLEY
Maybe.

BRIGIT
What's *he* doing tonight?

CHARLEY
They dunno yet. Probably fuckall. (*Turns out his pocket and shakes it.*) They don't have any bread either.

BRIGIT
You really want to go out with them?

CHARLEY
Well, we're not doing anything. I dunno, maybe a beer or two somewhere . . .

BRIGIT
I'm so tired . . .

CHARLEY
So sleep a little . . .

BRIGIT
I can't, not now.

CHARLEY
Nervous?

BRIGIT
No . . . not specially . . .

CHARLEY
Take some speed.

BRIGIT

I already took a couple today. You want one?

CHARLEY

It'd make me jittery.

BRIGIT

You're right, I'll take one more . . . just one . . . I
wanted to take one, that's why I got the Pepsi . . .
(CHARLEY *puts on a Wilson Pickett LP, turns it up, but
not quite high enough to drown the dialogue. With a
sudden spurt of energy, he hops and moves around the
room, singing with the music.*)

BRIGIT

(*Sourly.*) *You're* all right, aren't you?
(*No answer. He drums on the table and dances.*)

BRIGIT

(*Louder.*) I can't *stand* that Wilson Pickett any more!

CHARLEY

You just don't dig him yet!

BRIGIT

Ha, *ha.*

CHARLEY

(*Putting on the style.*) Heyy . . . I'm livin' again! (*Laughing maliciously.*) Don't need nothin' else . . . (*Smirking,
spins away from her.*)

BRIGIT

(*Trying to chill his exuberance.*) Don't you have anything
I can *read?*

CHARLEY

(*Picks up a book as he dances, pitches it to her.*) Norman
Mailer . . .

BRIGIT

(*Letting the book fall at her feet.*) He's a bore . . . (CHARLEY *ignores her. She says it louder.*) He's a BORE . . . (*Kicks the book under the bed.*)

CHARLEY

You flipped, or what? (*Singing, drumming again, he picks up another book from the table.*) The de-VINE . . . MarQUIIIIIS—(*Spins past her, drops the book in her lap.*)

BRIGIT

(*Picks up the book, goes to the gram, turns it down a bit.*) De Sade . . . (*With a bored air, opens the book and reads sarcastically.*) . . . and I discharged upon her . . . and I discharged upon her . . . (*Turns a page.*) . . . and I discharged upon her . . . (*Turns a page.*) . . . and I discharged upon her . . . (*Sighs.*) A little monotonous, isn't it? (*Drops the book on the floor.*)

CHARLEY

(*Still dancing, crooning the music.*) I told you, read the Norman Mailer! It's good!

BRIGIT

The great American statue who's seen a lot of pigeons. No, thanks. (*Smirking at him.*) *You* could write something . . . for a change . . .

CHARLEY

Not while the *mu*-sic's going, man . . . oooo . . . listen to that . . . (*Drums again.*) Tatatata . . . (*In rhythm.*) Watcha want me to *write* . . . watcha want me to *write* . . . write . . . write . . . write . . .

BRIGIT

You're an idle bastard.

CHARLEY

Listen, listen . . . I'll write a play . . . two people on the

stage . . . listening to records . . . one *record* . . . and
then another *record* . . . (*Drums again.*)

BRIGIT
Ha, *ha.*

CHARLEY
And right *there* . . . (*Points*) is this professor . . . with a
bi-i-ig diagram of the . . . the nervous system . . . right?
And he's explaining what the music . . . *does* to it . . .
right? And he's sort of singing what he says . . . like it was
set to music . . .

BRIGIT
You don't have a single idea, do you?

CHARLEY
(*Stung.*) Maybe *you* should write the fucking play.

BRIGIT
Maybe I should.

CHARLEY
I've got plenty of ideas.

BRIGIT
All you've got is bullshit.

CHARLEY
Hey, you're right . . . you know you're right? 'Cause
everything is bullshit . . .

BRIGIT
Oh, sure . . .

CHARLEY
Life is a *habit* . . . like smoking cigarettes!

BRIGIT
I've heard that before . . . it's one of your bullshit poems.

CHARLEY

(*Sits at the typewriter, flicks off the phonograph, blows the dust off the machine.*) What about this . . . the driving force in this world . . . is constipation! Whatever way you turn it . . . it's still a lot of shit!

(BRIGIT *clucks and closes her eyes in disgust.*)
Wait a minute, what about this? If you wanta make it, man . . . you do as *little* as possible . . . as *fast* as possible . . .

BRIGIT

It doesn't even rhyme.

CHARLEY

Blank verse!

BRIGIT

It's blank, all right. Shouldn't you exercise your brilliant intellect on the problem of what we're going to do tonight?

CHARLEY

I'm staying in . . . I'll get some writing done . . .

BRIGIT

You can write *now!*

CHARLEY

(*Shrugs, gets up.*) Ahh, I dunno . . .

BRIGIT

(*Irritated.*) But of course you'll know tonight . . .

CHARLEY

Sure, sure . . .

BRIGIT

Why'm I always so *tired* . . . I could sleep all day . . .

CHARLEY

All right, so sleep! Or go out and do some work or something . . .

BRIGIT

I can't even *think* about working . . . impossible . . . I mean, I *feel* all right, but I just don't want to *do* anything . . .

CHARLEY

Oh, don't be such a drag!

BRIGIT

What do you want? *I* can't do anything about it!

CHARLEY

So I'm a drag, too, right?

BRIGIT

Dunno. I mean, you don't give a shit about me.

CHARLEY

Yeah, well, unfortunately I do. That's what knocks me out.

BRIGIT

Oh, sure.

CHARLEY

No, really!

BRIGIT

(*Mocks him.*) Really!

CHARLEY

Hey, let's go for a walk . . .

BRIGIT

You go. I'll stay here.

CHARLEY

Oh, cute. Very cute.

BRIGIT

Or maybe I'll go home.

CHARLEY
What for?

BRIGIT
Just lay around, I guess . . .
(*She is on the bed.* CHARLEY *lies down beside her, embraces her.*)

BRIGIT
(*Fends him off.*) No . . . I don't feel like fucking, either . . .

CHARLEY
So drink something, then. (*Stung again, gets up and puts another LP on, something slow.*)

BRIGIT
God, we *can't* keep this up!

CHARLEY
But we *are* keeping it up . . . or are we?

BRIGIT
I don't even want to kill myself any more . . . I mean . . . somehow I feel . . . I feel really good . . . (*Pause.*) I don't look so bad today, do I?

CHARLEY
Like a real tart.

BRIGIT
Thank you very much.

CHARLEY
Slick, and smooth, and bright, and merry, and gay . . .

BRIGIT
God, you are stupid . . .
(CHARLEY *goes out of the room.*)

BRIGIT
Where you going?

CHARLEY
(*Off.*) The bog.

BRIGIT
Don't get any ideas in there . . .

CHARLEY
(*Off.*) (*Melodramatic voice.*) Do not deceive me while I am away . . .

BRIGIT
What difference would it make to you? (*Pause.*) When'd Joe say he was coming?

CHARLEY
(*Off.*) What?

BRIGIT
When is Joe coming?

CHARLEY
(*Off.*) He didn't say. (*Pause.*) Hey! It's gonna rain. The clouds are as black as a witch's bum out there.

BRIGIT
I still want to go *out* tonight . . .

CHARLEY
(*Off.*) We'll see. (*Toilet flushes. He comes in.*) I *do* believe, there's gonna be a storm.

BRIGIT
Charley, when did Joe say he was coming?

CHARLEY
If he's coming, it won't be long.

BRIGIT
With Monika? Or not?

CHARLEY
Don't ask me . . . if they haven't had a fight, I suppose he'll bring Monika. (*Goes to the window.*) Come the first of July, *I* am pissing off to Spain . . . whatever happens.

BRIGIT
And what am I supposed to do?

CHARLEY
Come along . . .

BRIGIT
Oh, sure . . . beautiful . . . and who'll pay the fare? Not Mummy, that's for sure.

CHARLEY
Something'll turn up. Your old lady ought to give you something . . . she's got enough bloody bread . . .

BRIGIT
Turn up from where, I'd like to know . . . at least you'll have the car, I hope.

CHARLEY
Yeah, I hope . . . I'm not bloody hitching . . .

BRIGIT
Why not?

CHARLEY
Do me a favor.

BRIGIT
You're just too fucking idle . . .

CHARLEY
Sure.

BRIGIT
Well, you are!

CHARLEY
Okay, I'm too fucking idle . . . (*Yawns.*)
    (*Outside, a car goes by.*)

BRIGIT
That could be Joe!

CHARLEY
(*Goes to the window.*) Uh-uh.

BRIGIT
(*Smugly.*) But it *was* a Volkswagen.

CHARLEY
(*Quiz-show manner.*) Give that lady a big . . . black . . .
CIGAR! Now would you like to try for something . . .
mmmm . . . nicer?

BRIGIT
Hey . . . does Joe know you've been fucking Monika?

CHARLEY
Uh huh. He more or less knows what's going on.

BRIGIT
Of course you told him . . .

CHARLEY
Of course.

BRIGIT
God, you're like a couple of old biddies gossiping over the
back fence!

CHARLEY
So? So we talk over things for a couple of hours? (*Pause.*)
It's sort of interesting the way all these little things get
around . . .

BRIGIT
Madly.

CHARLEY
Everybody *tangled* up with everybody else . . . ha!

BRIGIT
(*Pause.*) Christ, I'll be glad to get out of this shitbag!

CHARLEY
You're not the only one.

BRIGIT
Jesus, I've got to pee again . . .

CHARLEY
I vote we stay in tonight . . .

BRIGIT
Well, we'll just see . . . I wouldn't count on it . . . (*Goes out.*)
    (*A clap of thunder outside.*)

CHARLEY
There she goes! (*Calls.*) Hey, close the window in there! (*Goes to the mirror, looks at himself, examines his teeth, touches up his hair.*)
    (*Toilet flushes.* BRIGIT *comes in.*)

BRIGIT
If it rains we can go in Joe's car.

CHARLEY
Who said Joe was coming?

BRIGIT
I thought you said . . . he said he was coming . . .

CHARLEY
Did I said he said? Did I, did I? (*Pulls her down onto the bed. They begin some heavy smooching, which gets pas-*

sionate. *He reaches out from the bed and puts on another record. Thunder outside.*) Music . . . hath charms . . . to rrrrRRRRRRROUSE the savage beast . . .

(BRIGIT *has her T shirt off. He grabs her in a tight embrace. She works his belt buckle loose. They are very excited. He tries to undo the top button of her Levi's and can't with one hand.*)

BRIGIT
(*Gasping.*) Let me . . .
(*Undoes the button.* CHARLEY *undoes the zip and thrusts his hand into her Levi's. She moans and clutches at him. Outside, a car pulls up and beeps twice.*)

CHARLEY
(*Trying to untangle himself.*) Wait . . .

BRIGIT
(*Dizzy with passion.*) It's only Joe . . . (*Tries to hold* CHARLEY *down on her.*)

CHARLEY
(*Pulls away from her.*) Wait a minute . . . (*Goes to the window and whistles sharply.*)

BRIGIT
(*Panting furiously.*) God . . . you *bastard!*

JOE
(*Off.*) Hey hey!

CHARLEY
Hang on, I'll throw the key down!

JOE
Hey, man . . . am I interrupting anything?

CHARLEY
You're joking . . . (*Throws the key.*) Come on up.

BRIGIT

(*Flushed, trembling.*) Would you like me to get dressed?

CHARLEY

(*Raked by the contempt in her voice, avoids looking at her.*) Suit yourself.

>(BRIGIT *simply slips down under the covers. Brilliant flash of lightning outside and loud thunder.* CHARLEY *puts on another LP and* JOE *comes in.*)

JOE

Hey, man!

>(*Lights a cigarette, wanders around the room.* CHARLEY *does the same.* JOE *nods at the phonograph, snaps his fingers at the music.*)

Nice . . .

CHARLEY

Fan-tastic.

JOE

You know the new Jimmy Brown?

CHARLEY

I heard it.

JOE

Better than Wilson Pickett . . . not the band, but him.

CHARLEY

Yeah?

BRIGIT

So where's Monika?

JOE

That new boutique . . . I've got to pick her up.

CHARLEY

What'd you do last night, then?

JOE

Pogo took us down to the Armpit. They have a new show there. (*Makes a slurping noise.*) Tits! Lots of tits!

CHARLEY

(*Sniggering.*) I heard that wasn't all.

JOE

Yeah, well, they were going to do this thing, see . . . they had this fantastic tart, she weighs about eighteen stone . . . and they were going to do this thing with a goat, you know? But someone told Jimmy the fuzz were going to raid the place, and he chickened out.

CHARLEY

You sure it was Jimmy that chickened out, and not the goat?

JOE

Eighteen stone, baby! Tits like truck tires! Anyway, then we bumped into my brother. He took us out for some drag racing. Man, that is out of sight! Our new thing, you know?

CHARLEY

I thought your brother was always taking off somewhere?

JOE

Yeah . . . he's getting really wild. He'll be all right.

CHARLEY

Sure, why not?

JOE

So where were *you* yesterday?

CHARLEY

We were . . . uh . . . hey, what'd we do yesterday?

BRIGIT

(*Sourly.*) We were *here*.

CHARLEY

No, we weren't . . . wait, that was the day before . . . yeah, day before, we were at Pogo's.

JOE

What's Pogo up to?

CHARLEY

He's doing all right, I guess. His bird was there. He's just . . . painting his pictures.

BRIGIT

Did Monika get back today?

JOE

Uh huh. This morning.

CHARLEY

So how are . . . things?

JOE

Oh, you know . . . the same . . . same shit. You writing anything?

CHARLEY

Naah . . . not really.

JOE

What the hell *is* there to write? Man, I'm dried up . . . just nothing . . .

(CHARLEY *laughs.*)

JOE

You know, if we could write something . . . something really wild, you know? Like . . . like we're talking now, you know what I mean? Something like that . . . really nice . . . or else . . .

CHARLEY

Right . . . right!

JOE

Listen . . . really now . . . what are we doing tonight?

CHARLEY

No idea.

JOE

No decent movies on . . . anyway, I don't feel like a movie . . .

BRIGIT

There's nothing on at all.

CHARLEY

Nah, I checked it all . . . nothing. Not even a shitty movie.

BRIGIT

There's *The Swedish Au Pair* . . . nothing.

JOE

Hey man, did you see that one at the Rialto before?

CHARLEY

The Lash Cuts Deep?

JOE

About the nymphomaniac farm girl . . .

CHARLEY

And the masochistic horse . . .

JOE

Right! Right!

CHARLEY

I heard about it.

JOE

So . . . shall I come by later?

BRIGIT

You going already?

JOE
I've gotta pick up Monika.

BRIGIT
Anyway, come by . . .

CHARLEY
Or call up . . .
(*Thunder outside.*)

BRIGIT
Or we'll call up.

JOE
No, I won't be home.

CHARLEY
Fine . . . okay, then . . .

JOE
Okay . . . I'll call . . .
(*But he doesn't leave. He and* CHARLEY *shuffle around.*)

JOE
Hey, what time is it?

CHARLEY
I dunno, my watch is . . .
(*Dials "time" and hands* JOE *the receiver.*)

JOE
(*Listening.*) Peep-peep-peep—(*Drops the phone on the hook.*) Okay. So . . . do I come by? I mean, I don't mind, it's on the way.

BRIGIT
Come by.

JOE
Okay. I'll come by.

CHARLEY
Yeah, come by. Just in case.

JOE
Hey, are the parents back yet?

CHARLEY
Today or tomorrow. I dunno.

JOE
Too bad. We could have done something at the house.

CHARLEY
Yeah, well . . . (*Shrugs.*)

JOE
Well, I'll come by . . . just in case.

CHARLEY
Right.

BRIGIT
Make sure we're in.

JOE
Yeah, I'll call. *Ciao.*

CHARLEY
You don't have to call. Just come by.

JOE
Yeah, okay. If anything exciting's happening.

CHARLEY
Just come by.

JOE
Okay, I will. *Ciao.* (*Goes out.*)

CHARLEY
(*Calls after him.*) Hey, the key!

JOE
(*Off.*) I'll stick it in the mailbox!

CHARLEY
Right!
(*Goes to the window as another clap of thunder sounds. The car starts outside. Shouts down.*)
You don't have to call, okay?

JOE
(*Off, through noise of motor.*) No, I'll come by!

CHARLEY
(*Closes the window.*) It's going to piss down all night. My God, the *smoke* in here!

BRIGIT
Let some air in!
(CHARLEY *opens the window wide. The sound of rain outside. He puts another record on.* BRIGIT *crawls out of bed.*)
I'm going to take a shower.
(*Goes out. The telephone rings.*)

CHARLEY
(*Picks up the receiver.*) Hel-lo . . . What? Who? Who am I? Why, lady, I'm the fucking Pope!
(*Looks at the receiver, hangs up.*)

BRIGIT
(*Comes back in.*) Who was that?

CHARLEY
Wrong number.

BRIGIT
No hot water.

CHARLEY
Oh, no!

BRIGIT
Trickle, trickle . . . all gone.

(*A long scene in dumbshow. Both of them loaf around the room reading or leafing through magazines, scanning record sleeves. A record plays softly. After a routine embrace by the bed they begin to dance. They laugh at each other maliciously.* CHARLEY *lolls out his tongue and tries to kiss her. She dodges and pokes him in the belly. They dance on, regarding each other through half-closed eyes. They play elaborately at a jokey hostility which is becoming genuine.* CHARLEY *aims a light slap at her and she ripostes. He feigns injury, dancing grotesquely, and she scratches the back of his flopping hand. He slaps her lightly but angrily. She turns and wiggles her bum at him and he kicks her lightly. She staggers, whirls, and scratches him with some force on the upper arm and they dance some more,* CHARLEY *briefly inspecting his arm. He dodges like a boxer larking about and then suddenly gives her a ringing slap. She staggers back, and after a moment's shock, screams:*)

BRIGIT
You *cocksucker!*

(*She attacks him furiously, slapping, scratching. He smothers her in bedclothes. She falls, grabs a bottle and wings it at him, grazing him.* CHARLEY *puts on a Wilson Pickett LP, and as she disentangles herself, approaches her, smiling, and thumps her again. She claws his face. He howls in pain and goes to the mirror to inspect the deep scratches.*)

CHARLEY

Right.

(*Now a real fight, with* BRIGIT *screaming loudly and* CHARLEY *swearing.*)

CHARLEY

You pig, you twat, you bloody little *bitch*, you fucking *cow*, you *cunt!* (*Matching epithets to blows, he fells her with the last one.*) Now you crawl out of here! Rub your fucking tits along the floor and fucking *crawl!*

(*Kicks her. She drags herself to the bed, sobbing convulsively.* CHARLEY *sits down and lights a cigarette, trembling so badly that he drops it twice. N.B. This fight must be long, harsh, loud, and violent, including pauses for panting, and end brutally.*)

CHARLEY

(*Pacing quickly up and down.*) What do you always want to start scratching for? I told you last time that if you scratched me again . . . (*Pause.*) I don't even look what I'm doing . . . I don't look . . . you get me?

BRIGIT

Gimme a cigarette.

CHARLEY

(*Lights another cigarette, pats her on the back.*) There. (*Gives her the cigarette over her shoulder.*) We'll take a walk, okay? (*Goes to the window. The rain has stopped.*) Even if it does start to rain again. There it goes . . . (*Rain outside. Pause.*) Fucking piss-ass weather.

(BRIGIT *gets up and begins to dress.*)

CHARLEY

What are you getting dressed for?

BRIGIT

(*Screams.*) Because I want to dress, you stupid asshole!

CHARLEY

Okay . . . okay . . .

(BRIGIT *goes to the telephone and dials.*)

CHARLEY

I hope he's home . . .

BRIGIT

Get away . . .

CHARLEY

Who you calling, then?

BRIGIT

Hello . . . may I speak to Eddie, please? What . . . yes
. . . yes . . . this is Brigit . . . when? I see. No, nothing
special. No, it's not important. Just say I called to say hello.
Yes . . . what? Oh, yes, please. (*Pause.*) Yes, I'll wait.

CHARLEY

Isn't Eddie there? Is Eddie-teddie-weddie gone to beddie-
bye? Without his sweetie pie?

BRIGIT

(*To* CHARLEY.) Oh, you'll see . . .

CHARLEY

Is he there?

BRIGIT

(*Pause.*) Hello? (*Sweetly.*) Hi, Eddie! Fine, lovely. How
are you? Yes . . . mmmm . . . oh, I'd like that . . .

CHARLEY

(*Loudly.*) He better pick you up from here right away!

BRIGIT

(*Covers the mouthpiece.*) Sorry, what? . . . What?

CHARLEY

(*Loudly.*) Next gentleman, please!

BRIGIT

No . . . of course not!

CHARLEY

Tell him he'd better pick you up right away!

BRIGIT

(*To* CHARLEY.) Will you shut up? (*To the telephone.*)
No, not you. What?

CHARLEY

While you're still hot and wet!

BRIGIT

. . . No . . . at Charley's place . . . yes . . . no!

CHARLEY

Because I'm going to kick your ass out of here!

BRIGIT

(*Angrily into the phone.*) Yes, at Charley's place. So? Oh,
now, come *on!* But . . . look, are you coming or not?

CHARLEY

Tell him not to be such a prick!

BRIGIT

I *know* I haven't called for a long time . . .

CHARLEY

(*Childish nasal voice.*) Doesn't he WANNA come?

BRIGIT

(*Into the phone.*) Oh, God, you're so *silly!* No! No . . .
no . . . no . . . you drive to the cemetery . . . you
know . . . and then take the first left . . .

CHARLEY

Left into Rutland Avenue and the third house on the
right . . .

BRIGIT
Oh, sure. (*Gets up.*) Let me out . . .

CHARLEY
You really want to go?
 (*Sound of* JOE's *Volkswagen outside.*)

BRIGIT
Is that Joe?

CHARLEY
(*Goes to the window.*) Yeah . . .

BRIGIT
Perfect . . . I can go with him . . .

CHARLEY
(*Whistles out the window, then takes* BRIGIT *by the arm.*)
Come on . . . out the back a second . . . come *on* . . .
 (*He takes her out. After a moment* MONIKA *comes in.*
 She lights a cigarette and sits on the bed. Then she goes
 out to the toilet. JOE *comes in.*)

JOE
Monika?

MONIKA
(*Off.*) Just coming . . .
 (JOE *takes off his jacket, opens his shirt and pulls it out*
 of his pants, picks up a bottle, picks up a mashed hat from
 the floor and puts it on, and regards himself in the mirror.
 MONIKA *comes back in.*)

MONIKA
Anything to drink?

JOE
Gin?
 (*Offers her the bottle.*)

MONIKA
Not for me.

JOE
You like my hat?

MONIKA
You look like the village idiot.

JOE
Try it . . .

MONIKA
Knock it off . . .

JOE
(*Jams the hat down over her ears.*) Ha!

MONIKA
(*Rips off the hat and throws it away.*) Cretin. (*Pause.*) So where are they?

JOE
They wanted to go for a walk . . .

MONIKA
(*Picks up a book, amused.*) Since when does Charley read Wittgenstein?

JOE
He wants to improve his mind . . . anything wrong with that? (*Mockingly.*) It's beautiful to improve your mind . . .

MONIKA
Don't be so snotty . . .

JOE
Yeah, man . . . Wittgenstein . . . (*Takes off his pants, gets into bed, picks up a book.*)

MONIKA
When are they coming back?

JOE
Dunno.

MONIKA
Did Charley thump her?

JOE
Could be . . .

MONIKA
Just to show how masculine he is . . .

JOE
Uh huh . . . you ought to know . . .

MONIKA
He wasn't quite as floppy as you thought, either . . .

JOE
I hope not.

MONIKA
He was a little limp at first . . . but if I remember, he was
horny enough . . . in the end.

JOE
In the *end*? Oh, like that, was it? (*No reaction from*
MONIKA.) Put on some Wilson Pickett, hey . . . and slip
into something more comfortable?

MONIKA
(*Puts the LP on, strips off most of her clothes to the music,
and slips into bed with* JOE.) Very well, your Grace . . .
away we *gooo* . . .

JOE
(*Nervous.*) A little less mouth, okay? Turn it up, please?

MONIKA
(*Lifts up the covers to look.*) Oh, my, we're not up at all,
are we?
   (JOE *grabs down the covers.* MONIKA *smirks.*)
Don't be nervous now . . . no excuses . . . do it now or
neverrr . . .
   (*Pause. Then cuttingly:*)
Oooo, ba . . . beee . . . poochiewoochie teddybear can
come and get his honey-woney . . . ooooh, teddy isn't go-
ing to ravish me?
   (*She is still groping.* JOE *thumps her with his elbow to
   make her stop and move away.*)
OooooooOOOOOooooo . . . bang bang goes the little
teddybear . . . bang bang with his *el*-bow . . . is that all
teddybear can bang bang with? Hmmm? Hmmm?
Hmmmm? (*Gropes.*)

JOE
Wait a *minute* . . . suppose someone comes in?
   (MONIKA *scratches him.*)

JOE
Ow! (*Pause. He grabs her breast.*) My God! Polystyrene!
   (MONIKA *grabs too, under the covers.* JOE *doubles up
   suddenly.*)
Owww, *Christ!*
   (*They begin to scuffle and fight, entangled in the bed-
   clothes. The struggle gets rough.*)
Don't *do* that . . .
   (*Thumps* MONIKA'S *head, which is covered by the
   blanket.*)

MONIKA
(*Screams furiously.*) OWWWWWWW! (*Emerges with
blood pouring from her nose.*) Oh . . . God . . . my
nose . . .

JOE

Lemme see . . . (*Tries to look, but she has her hands over her face.*) Wait, get your hands away . . . get your *hands* away . . .

MONIKA

You son of a *bitch* . . .

JOE

Hey, you think it's broken? (*She sobs. He reaches out and touches the nose. She screams loudly.*) Yep . . . broken, all right.

MONIKA

Take me to the doctor . . . right *now!*

JOE

Right, right . . . I couldn't really see what I was doing, see . . . (*Paces, nervous and angry.*) Come on, get something on . . .

MONIKA

Oooohhhh . . . *God* . . . (*Moans and sobs.*)

JOE

Does it hurt there, too?

MONIKA

Yes, it hurts . . . give me my *blouse* . . .

JOE

I better take you to the hospital . . .

MONIKA

Not the accident hospital . . . I'll have to wait . . . oh . . . *God* . . .

JOE

No, no, the City Hospital . . . the emergency department

. . . . (*Hesitates as she sobs.*) Hey, maybe I better call up first . . .

MONIKA

All right . . . call . . . damn . . .

JOE

Or maybe . . . maybe we should just go down there . . . no, I better call up . . .

MONIKA

Call up, you silly bastard! Make sure the doctor's there!

JOE

The doctor's *there* . . . I mean, it's a hospital . . . they've got all kinds of doctors there . . . we'll just go . . .

MONIKA

Ring . . . up! (*Grabs the telephone.*) At least look up the number, if you're too stupid to call up! (*Joe riffles in the phone book.*) It's the *City* Hospital.

JOE

All right, all right . . . what do you think I'm looking up, the police?

MONIKA

You can look them up, too.

JOE

(*Looks at her.*) Yeah, well . . . how do we say it happened?

MONIKA

Will you find the *number?*

JOE

Wait . . . City . . . *Hospital* . . .

MONIKA

Give me the *number* . . .

JOE

859-2822. (MONIKA *dials.*) But don't say how it happened . . .

MONIKA

Emergency department, please . . . a broken nose . . . yes . . . a *smashed* nose . . . (*Sobs.*)

JOE

Come on, we'll drive down . . . there'll be a doctor there . . . come on . . . (MONIKA *slams the phone down, stands up.*) . . . It'll be all right, babe . . . (*Puts out his cigarette.*)

MONIKA

Let's go *now*, then!
(*A whistle from outside in the street.*)

JOE

Hang on, I'll see who it is . . . (*Goes to the window and whistles.*)

CHARLEY

(*Outside.*) Joe?

JOE

Hey, man!

CHARLEY

Wanna go for a beer?

JOE

Not now, man . . . we got . . . just a second, I'll come down . . .

MONIKA

Go on!

CHARLEY

What is it?

JOE

Monika's nose is broken . . .

CHARLEY

Her nose is broken?

JOE

Right . . . we've gotta get down to the emergency department . . . hang on . . . (*Quickly crosses the room.*) Let's go, come on . . .
(*They go out and down the stairs. We hear them meet the others and exchange a few muffled words.*)

CHARLEY

(*Enters.*) Jesus, look at all the blood! (BRIGIT *comes in.*) They're out of their minds . . .

BRIGIT

(*Mildly excited.*) I had no idea that Joe was such a . . . brute!

CHARLEY

He said he didn't mean to . . . it was an accident . . . you know . . . zap . . . before you even know what happens . . . boom . . . I can just imagine . . .

BRIGIT

Three cheers . . .

CHARLEY

You like it? I can do it too.
(BRIGIT *laughs.* CHARLEY *pinches her from behind.*)
You don't think so? (*Kicks her half hard on the bottom, laughs as she slaps him.*)

BRIGIT

I just wish I knew what I saw in you.

CHARLEY
(*Pokes her in the breast.*) Not a thing . . . but . . . you
fancy me. Madly. (*Boxes around her casually.*) You fancy
me madly . . . (*Keeps boxing.*)

BRIGIT
Will you *stop* it?
(*He boxes harder, she scratches him, he hits her, she falls
on the bed, throws a book at him, he throws a book back
and the ensuing book fight becomes increasingly* light-
hearted.)

BRIGIT
(*Throws a book.*) Shitgenstein . . .

CHARLEY
(*Ripostes.*) Harold Pinter-*shit!*

BOTH
(*Ad lib, hurling books back and forth.*) Scott Fitzgerald-
shit, Edward Albee-*shit*, D. H. Lawrence-*shit*, Tennessee
Williams-*shit*, Sigmund Freud-*shit*, William Burroughs-*shit*,
William Shakespeare-*shit*, Dostoevski-*shit*, Ronald Laing-
shit, Henry Miller-*shit*, Edward Bond-*shit*, Wilhelm Reich-
shit, Arthur Miller-*shit*, Gertrude Stein-*shit*, Jean Genet-
shit, Norman Mailer-*shit*, Samuel Beckett-*shit*, Bertrand
Russell-*shit*, C. G. Jung-*shit*, Jean-Paul Sartre-*shit*, Marshall
McLuhan-*shit*, John Osborne-*shit*, William Faulkner-*shit*,
Ernest Hemingway-*shit*, Holy Bible-*shit*, etc., etc., etc.
(*In high spirits, but not affectionately, they stand laughing at each other across the chaotic room.* CHARLEY *puts
on a loud record, conducts with both arms, lurching
among the rubbish, kicking things around.*)

CHARLEY
Ba-badoob-mbee-*baaa* . . . hey . . . hey . . .

BRIGIT

(*Shouting through the music.*) Charley! Charley! Can't we clean up this *mess?*

CHARLEY

(*Flings the bedclothes on the floor.*) You're putting me *on* . . .
    (*Both of them smoke, moving around the room, steamed up, nervous. Not a word is spoken.*)

CHARLEY

Any booze left?

BRIGIT

Some gin, I think . . .

CHARLEY

Bring it out! Man . . . I want to get *smashed* . . . man, I'm . . . I dunno . . .

BRIGIT

You're what? Up tight?

CHARLEY

Yeah . . . up tight . . . but wild, you know? I can feel all my nerves, you know? All together . . . vibrating . . . get the gin, sweetheart . . .
    (BRIGIT *goes out.* CHARLEY *hops grotesquely to the music, falls heavily, howls, smothering the cry in the bedclothes.*)
Bring a glass!

BRIGIT

(*Enters with bottle and glass.*) There.

CHARLEY

You have one too . . .

BRIGIT

There's some champagne out there . . . I thought maybe you were saving it . . .

CHARLEY

Saving bullshit! Drink it! Drink it all!
(BRIGIT *goes out for the champagne.* CHARLEY *guzzles the gin.*)

BRIGIT

(*Brings in the champagne.*) Will you open it? (CHARLEY *gives her a friendly kiss, slips behind her, and pops the cork at her bum. She ignores it, smoking calmly.* CHARLEY *gives her back the bottle.*) Is Joe coming back?

CHARLEY

I guess so . . . not Monika, though, that's for sure . . .

BRIGIT

Then he should be here pretty soon . . .

CHARLEY

Uh huuuuh . . . (*Paces up and down.*) Hey, what do you say . . . we have a . . . suicide pact?

BRIGIT

Not for me. But you go right ahead.

CHARLEY

C'mon . . . we'll *slide* into a nice, hot bath, right? And open up each other's arteries . . . right? Kkkkkkkkk! See, you *slide* into a nice, hot bath . . . because it doesn't hurt that way, right? I mean, I read about it . . . and then you *ssslice* 'em open . . . kkkkkkkkkk!

BRIGIT

Come on, Charley . . . let's clean up . . .

CHARLEY

'D I ever tell you about how Conrad wanted to manufacture Teddy?

BRIGIT

(*Wearily.*) No . . .

CHARLEY

Man . . . what a groovy story that was . . . I could even write a play about it . . . you know Teddy, right?

BRIGIT

The painter?

CHARLEY

Uh huh. You know he used to make umbrellas? Hey. Pasty-faced son of a bitch . . . and Conrad and this other guy saw him one day down in the Art Club . . . and all of a sudden Conrad says . . . you know what? We're gonna *manufacture* him . . .

BRIGIT

What?

CHARLEY

Manufacture, see . . . really do it . . . he was going to *manufacture* Teddy into a big-deal artist, see . . . every-thing . . . work it all out so he was gonna be famous, right? . . . Then when they had him all made up, this fantastic product, you know, famous and all that shit . . . they were gonna fix it so he kkkkkkkk . . . farewell, cruel world, right? . . . But what happened, see . . . *Teddy* didn't do it . . . *Conrad* did it . . . (*Makes hanging ges-ture, tongue out.*) Kkkkkk! Isn't that wild? Not Teddy . . . Conrad!

BRIGIT

Uh huh.

CHARLEY

I mean, someone's gotta do it, right? That's the law of nature . . . sort of like . . . the sorcerer's apprentice, right? . . . so now *Teddy* is a big-deal famous artist . . . groovy character . . . that's the . . . law of nature, right? Two groovy characters . . . and the grooviest character wins . . . all bullshit . . . all nerves and bullshit. (*Goes to the window.*) Rain didn't cool it off . . . sultry out there . . . like a jungle . . . in here, too . . . real Tennessee Williams atmosphere . . . hey, hey!

BRIGIT

Ha, *ha*.

CHARLEY

One more shitty afternoon . . .

BRIGIT

Don't keep talking like that . . . if you could just for once try to . . .

CHARLEY

Shitty . . . but *intense* . . .

BRIGIT

That's not what I mean by intense . . . you always think everything you do is intense . . .

CHARLEY

So what? (*Pause.*) God, you are so . . . *thick* . . . sooooo fucking *thick* . . . I wish to Christ Joe would get back . . .

BRIGIT

Your sweet Joey-boy . . . you'd be lost without him, wouldn't you?

CHARLEY

I'd rather marry him than you.

BRIGIT

(*Laughs, embarrassed.*) Me, too.

CHARLEY

I just don't fancy you any more . . . all of a sudden I just don't fancy you any more . . .

BRIGIT

You think I fancy you?

CHARLEY

That's the *tragedy* of it . . . you do fancy me . . . you fancy me like a dog fancies a bone . . . you fancy me like mad . . . ah, ha . . . so *I* don't fancy *you* any *more* . . .

BRIGIT

That's all right with me. We can break it off . . .

CHARLEY

Break it off, break it off . . . how many times have I heard *that* shit . . . ah, ha . . . I don't *wanna* break it off and you're not *gonna* break it off . . . 's a very delicate distinction . . . an' you know that I need you . . . yeah . . . I'll be glad when I can get away out of here . . . best thing is to piss off right this minute . . . go to Formentera, see Carla . . .

BRIGIT

What's the *matter* with you all of a sudden?

CHARLEY

(*Mocks her tone.*) *Matter?* What the hell d'you think's the *matter?*

BRIGIT

Well, what?

CHARLEY

(*Pretty drunk.*) Yeah . . . today was just a little bit too much . . . doesn' matter, though . . . Carla is at least a

. . . an *agreeable person* . . . hardly even speaks English
. . . doesn't bullshit all the time . . . just . . . agreeable
. . . you dig? . . . agreeable . . . an *agreeable woman*
. . . no ulterior motives . . . you dig? . . . she's just . . .
there . . . doesn' *do* anything . . . an' that's what makes
her perfect . . . anyway, she's fucking sexy . . . Christ,
it was great . . . full of hash in the burning heat . . .
sweating like a bloody fucking . . . stallion . . . (*Takes
a quick turn around the room.*) You can piss off any time
you want to . . .

BRIGIT
Okay . . . (*Gets up.*) Joe can take me home . . .

CHARLEY
If he does . . . if he does, that's fine . . .

BRIGIT
(*Goes to* CHARLEY, *kisses him tenderly.*) My stupid
baby . . .

CHARLEY
(*Smiles, backs away a bit.*) Oh yeah . . . oh, yeah . . .
women . . . women really have it hard . . . they really
do have it hard . . .

BRIGIT
You can say that again . . .

CHARLEY
I was just discussing that very thing with Freddy . . .

BRIGIT
With Freddy . . .

CHARLEY
And he is also of the opinion . . . that women really do
have it very hard . . .

BRIGIT

(*Grabs him.*) Why are you so nasty all of a sudden?

CHARLEY

I *told* you how nasty I can get . . . just like that . . . and
now . . . I'm nasty . . . and it feels great!
　　(*Makes provocative movements.* JOE's *Volkswagen is
　　heard.*)

BRIGIT

There's Joe. I'll go down right now.

CHARLEY

Right, piss off . . .

BRIGIT

Are any of my things here?

CHARLEY

I dunno . . .

BRIGIT

(*Rummaging around.*) What?

CHARLEY

Out of it . . . (*Bellows suddenly.*) Piss off, damn you!
Fuck off out of here! Haven't you gone yet?
　　(BRIGIT *throws herself on the bed and weeps.* CHARLEY
　　puts on "Sergeant Pepper's Lonely Hearts Club Band."
　　JOE *enters.*)

CHARLEY

Hey, man . . . drink up! (*Gives him the bottle.*)

JOE

(*Takes it and drinks, nodding at* BRIGIT.) What's up with
her?

CHARLEY

Who knows, man . . . so what's new?

JOE

Nothing new, man . . . you know what happened . . .

CHARLEY

Broken nose . . .

JOE

Right . . .

CHARLEY

So? They didn't keep her in the hospital?

JOE

(*Tragic pose.*) Yes! (*Pause.*) My poor *love* . . . (*Smiles cynically but keeps the same tragic tone.*) My lovelovelove-loveloveloveloveloveloooooove . . .

CHARLEY

Yeah, man . . . not so simple . . . motherfucker . . . love . . .

JOE

(*Sings to the record.*) "Sergeant Pepper's Lonely Hearts Club Band" . . . man, when you think . . . when you think . . . there's one thing, man . . . there's just one thing that's really dangerous . . . *really* dangerous, you dig? . . . and that . . . is re-pro-fucktion . . . you dig me, man?

CHARLEY

I dig.

JOE

I dunno . . . I dunno . . . man, I am so *thirsty* . . .

CHARLEY

Drink up! (BRIGIT *sobs. He speaks to her in a friendly tone.*) Will you shut up? Come on, have some gin . . . (*Yells louder.*) HEY!

JOE

Hey, man . . . I got some stuff . . . if you wanna turn on . . .

CHARLEY

Who from?

JOE

Sonny gave it to me before he took off . . .

CHARLEY

Good stuff?

JOE

I made a joint with it last week . . . beautiful . . . not like that shit the time before . . .

CHARLEY

Let's roll one, man . . .

JOE

You wanna do it?

CHARLEY

Right . . . (*To* BRIGIT, *who is still on the bed.*) Hey, you got your nail scissors? (*She does not answer.* JOE *takes out the hash and cigarettes, and papers.* CHARLEY *speaks to* JOE.) Hang on, I'll get some scissors . . .

JOE

(*To* BRIGIT.) You gonna smoke? (*No reply.*)

CHARLEY

(*Brings in the scissors.*) It couldn't be a better day for it.

JOE

Man, we're halfway stoned already . . .

CHARLEY

(*Finishing the first joint.*) Looks good, man, looks good . . .

JOE

(*Slopes around the room, keeping time on his own head.*)
Right there . . . papapapapa . . . tatatapapa tatam! Tatam . . . ttm . . . (*Drums on the edge of a table . . .
faster and faster.*)

CHARLEY

Hey, we've got to put on something really groovy . . .
(JOE *drums away.*) Hey, put something on . . .

JOE

Right . . .

CHARLEY

Which one?

JOE

The Stones . . . something cool . . .
   (*Puts on "Back Street Girl." The cigarette is ready. In
   the stillness* BRIGIT *sits up on the bed and watches them
   with tear-filled eyes.*)

JOE

Go ahead, man . . .

CHARLEY

Right . . . matches . . . matches . . .

JOE

There . . .

CHARLEY

(*Before he lights up.*) You know Val got busted?

JOE

Yeah, I heard . . . up at Pete's place . . . they got everybody . . .

CHARLEY

Yeah, well, they were all stoned out of their minds . . . the fuzz were in before they knew what was happening . . . they got Danny too . . . poor fucker was on shit . . . he flipped, he just flipped . . . (*Lights up, inhales deeply.*) Beautiful, man . . . beautiful . . . (*Draws deep again, passes the joint to* JOE, *who also takes two deep drags. They smile at each other. The phonograph is turned up. Both rise and wander around.* BRIGIT *lights a cigarette and leans back.* CHARLEY *goes to the window.*) Wait, I'll close the window. (*Closes the shutters, then the window, turns on the light, and laughs to* JOE.)

JOE

You rolled a strong one, man . . .

CHARLEY

Right . . . plenty more where that came from . . . (*They pace, heads down.* BRIGIT *turns down the music.*)

CHARLEY

(*Gradually turning on.*) Beautiful . . . beautiful . . . out of sight . . .

JOE

Really out of sight . . . nothing wrong with this stuff, man . . .

CHARLEY

Wrooooong . . . he-heyyy . . .

JOE

Ga-dong dong . . . doooooong . . .
(*Both laugh briefly, then get hold of themselves and keep their cool. They move up and down, making slightly grotesque movements to the music, seeming gay but not really high. Cheerfully they smoke the cigarette to the end.*)

CHARLEY
(*To* BRIGIT.) Come on, try it . . .

BRIGIT
Joe can drive me home now . . .

JOE
Since when am I a taxi?

CHARLEY
Oh . . . *madame* . . . (*Bows low.*) The fucking subway is at your service . . .

BRIGIT
(*Lies down again, weeps.*) You mean bastards!

CHARLEY
This is groovy stuff . . .

JOE
Sonny got it really cheap . . .

CHARLEY
Where?

JOE
Dunno . . . a café in Istanbul or . . . somewhere in Turkey, I dunno . . . he's living off it now . . .

CHARLEY
Hey, that's beautiful . . . for an insurance man . . .

JOE
Not now, man . . . he switched . . . didn't like the office any more . . . didn't like that old death insurance . . . so he switched to happy-life insurance, dig?

CHARLEY
(*Laughs wildly.*) Happy . . . happyyyyy . . . hey, hey! Happy *all* the *time* . . . (*Laughs.*)

JOE

(*Takes it up.*) Happy *happy* hap hap . . . ba-dap *zap* . . . ba-dap . . . ba-dap *ba*-dap . . . bap-y-dap . . . happyyyyy . . .

CHARLEY

(*Does a kind of horsy dance around the room to the music.*) Ba-dap-y-*dap* giddyyap . . . giddy*ap* . . . bap bap . . . badapydappy dap dappy dap lappy lap lap hapalappy lap lap . . . (*Collapses in helpless laughter.*)

JOE

(*Rolling another joint.*) Nice walkies . . . nice horsie take a nice walkie talkies . . .

CHARLEY

(*Dancing.*) Happy *all* the time . . . ba-dime dime . . . ba-dime diiiime . . . (*Stumbles, falls.*)

JOE

Pigeon in the grass on your ass ass ass . . . (*Lights the joint.*) OOooooooo eeeeeeeeee . . . ba-doom doooooom . . .

CHARLEY

(*Gets up to take the joint.*) Boom boom boom . . . (*Deep drag.*) Boomy doom *doooooooom!* (*Pirouettes, letting out the smoke slowly.*)

JOE

Mooom . . . mooom . . . muuuusic . . . 'sgoing on forever . . . man . . . music's going on and on . . . and on . . .

CHARLEY

A-go *bye* . . . bye . . .

JOE

I know *why* . . . why . . .

CHARLEY
'Cause we're *high* . . . *high* . . .

JOE
A-know *why* . . . high . . .

CHARLEY
Die . . . die . . .

BOTH
Higher . . . higher . . . higher . . . higher . . . (*Dancing wildly, singing the words ad lib, but with strong rhythm, they whirl to the music, keeping time wildly, giggling, swooping at last to a staggering stop on either side of the bed where* BRIGIT *lies.*)

CHARLEY
(*Bends over unsteadily, pulls up the hem of* BRIGIT'*s* T *shirt to peer underneath. She slaps his hand away.* CHARLEY *wags his finger at* JOE.) Very short skirt . . .

JOE
That skirt . . . is a T . . . shirt!

CHARLEY
T . . . shirt, see shirt!

JOE
Me shirt, bee shirt . . .

CHARLEY
Shirty shirt shirt . . .

JOE
Titty shirt shirt . . . (*Makes an unsteady try at* BRIGIT'*s bust. She rolls onto her stomach.*)

CHARLEY
Shitty shirt shirt . . .

JOE
(*Catching the rhythm.*) *Shirty* shirt shirt . . .

CHARLEY
(*Pointing to* BRIGIT's *bum and silently clapping his hands.*)
Shitty shirt, *shitty* shirt, *shitty* shirt *shirt* . . .

BOTH
(*Pounding the rhythm on* BRIGIT's *bum,* JOE *with one hand,
the other holding the joint out of harm's way.*) *Shitty* shirt,
shitty shirt, *shitty* shirt *shirt* . . .

BRIGIT
(*Screams.*) Stop it! (*Turns and kicks, but they stagger back
out of range.*)

CHARLEY
(*Snapping fingers in rhythm.*) Well, buzz, *buzz,* cuz . . .
here come de *fuzz* . . .

JOE
(*Same rhythm.*) Yes he *does* . . . yes, he *does* . . .

CHARLEY
. . . fuzz fuzz *cuz* . . . buzz buzz *buzz* . . .

JOE
Fuzzl buzzl muzzl cuzzl . . .

CHARLEY
Duddy duzz *duzz* . . . cuzz, cuzz? Uzz? Uzz?

JOE
(*Pointing at* BRIGIT, *who has again rolled onto her stomach.*)
Guzz, *guzz!*

CHARLEY
(*Nodding cheerfully.*) Duzz *duzz!*

BOTH

(*Holding* BRIGIT *down and pounding her bum again in rhythm.*) Buzz, *buzz, here* come de *fuzz, duzz* cuzz *buzz? Duzz* he *duzz! Fuzzl* buzzl *wuzzl* cuzzl, duzzee duzz *duzz! Guzz,* cuzz, here come de *fuzz!* Here come de *fuzz!* Buzz duzz *duzz!* Fuzz fuzz *fuzz!* Duzz duzz *duzz* . . .

> (BRIGIT *kicks, screams, and they can't hold her. They stagger back and bawl in chorus, ignoring the record, singing.*)

We come from *Roe*-dean,
>   nice girls are weeeee . . .

We haven't *lost* our
>   vir-gin-ityyyyy . . .

(*They break into camp shrieks and giggles, flopping about; then, arms around each other's waist, bawl another song.*)

Sheeeeeeeeeee . . .
hasn't a spot on her character, no,
she hasn't a spot on her name . . .
she lives in a spot
not far from the spot
the spot that's called spottery lane . . .
Sheeeeeeeeeee's . . .
got spots on her fingers and spots on her toes,
and spots on the end of her nose . . .
but the most charming spot
is the spot that she's got
the spot on the end of her
>   toora-lye, tooralye, oora-lye . . . ayyyyye . . .

(*Now they howl war cries and shuffle around in the rubbish, grunting the nonsense in Indian rhythms.*)

Buzz, buzz, buzz, buzz, *fuzz,* uzz, uzz, uzz, *fuzz* buzz, *fuzz* buzz, *duzz,* uzz, uzz, uzz, *here* come de *fuzz,* here come de *fuzz,* here come de *fuzz,* de fuzz duzz *duzz,* fuzzl duzzl duzzl duzzl . . .

JOE

(*Wiggling index finger in his mouth, utters a loud war cry, then burbles like an idiot.*) b-b-b-b-b-b-b-b-b-b . . . g-g-g-g-g-g-g-g-g-g . . . b-b-b-b-b-b-b-beautiful . . . beautifooooooooooool . . .

CHARLEY

*Beau*tiful, *cutie*ful . . . suitiful . . . dutiful . . .

JOE

*Easy Ri*der . . . *die*der . . . *sli*der . . .

CHARLEY

(*Pulling eyes into slants, bowing, with Japanese accent.*) Ah, soo . . . you ah supprize I spik you *ran*gradge . . .

JOE

(*Pointing to* CHARLEY, *lisping.*) D'*you* love *me?*

CHARLEY

Kick him in the *knee!*

JOE

(*Campily furious.*) *You* love the *dolls!*

CHARLEY

Kick him in the *other* knee!

JOE

Muuuuuusic . . . muuuusic . . .

CHARLEY

It's a trick, man, a tricky trick trick . . .

JOE

Sicky sick *tricky* trick . . .

CHARLEY

Cha cha cha, sick sick,

JOE
*Ch*achacha, prick prick,

BOTH
*Ch*achacha dick dick, *cha*chacha sick sick, *cha*chacha lick
lick, *cha*chacha prick prick, *ha*haha dick dick, *cha*chacha
chick chick (*Very loud, rising to a climax*) *ga*gaga nick
nick, *cha*chacha *sick* sick, chacha *chow* dick, dick, *wow*-
owow ick ick, *wow*owow, *wow*owow WOWOWOW
WOWOWOW . . . (*Both reeling, staggering, yelling,
laughing hysterically. They face each other with open
arms.*)

JOE
Old darling!

CHARLEY
Old fruit!
   (*They embrace and kiss each other deeply on the mouth.*
   BRIGIT *runs into the kitchen.*)

JOE
Wass the matter with *her?* Doesn't like to see the fellas
kiss . . . fellas are beautiful . . . beautiful thing in the
whoooooole world . . .

CHARLEY
Beautifuller than the . . . beautiful . . . (*Takes a globe
of the world out of the wardrobe, takes the sphere out of
its frame, and throws it to* JOE.) Catch!

JOE
The world . . . is really . . . all . . . fucked up . . .
(*They both gape silently at the globe.*)

CHARLEY
(*Dreamily.*) S'beautiful . . .

JOE

Ah, you're flipped!

CHARLEY

Look, man . . . beauuuuutiful . . .

JOE

I think . . . I think . . . I'm gonna trash this world . . .
right down the shithole . . . with all the other shit . . .

CHARLEY

(*Holding his nose, speaking as though he had a cold.*) The
pladet has had it . . . how sad it will be . . . and now we
will bury it down in the seeeeeaa . . .
(*They troop gaily out with the globe.*)

JOE

(*Outside in the bog.*) Byyyyyyeee world!

CHARLEY

(*Softer.*) Bye-eye . . . (*There is a splash, then the flushing
of the toilet.*) It won't goooo! (*Chants.*) The world is moving on the face of the waaa . . . terrs . . .

JOE

It won't *go* . . .

CHARLEY

(*Chants.*) As it was in the beginning . . .

JOE

(*Chants.*) . . . is now . . .

CHARLEY

(*Chants.*) . . . and ever shaaalll beeeee . . . *ha,* ha!

JOE

(*Chants.*) . . . shaaall beeee . . . *ha,* ha!

BOTH

(*Chanting.*) Shaaalll beee, *ha,* ha! Shaaalll beee, *ha,* ha! Shaaalll beee, *ha,* ha! Shaaalll beee, *ha,* ha! (*They laugh and come back in.*)

CHARLEY

I'm . . . *observing* myself again . . . when I get stoned . . . I'm always *observing* myself . . .

JOE

It's a stake-out, man!

CHARLEY

Buzz, buzz, here come de fuzz . . . (*Giggles.*)

JOE

Man, that record is so slooow . . . sooo slooooww . . .

CHARLEY

You just wanna stand . . . dig? . . . just stand for a while, right there . . . don' dance! . . . an' then . . . after while . . . then you flip around . . . (*Pirouettes*) like this . . . (*Holds a grotesque pose*) that's the new thing, man!

JOE

Where're those comic books, man? I wanna look at that groovy one . . .

CHARLEY

Zap? Mister Natural? Yellow Dog?

JOE

No, man . . . that other one . . . what was it?

CHARLEY

Captain Guts? Little Johnny Fuckerfaster?

JOE

There was this little creep in it, with the gigantic cock . . .

CHARLEY

Old Uncle Uh-Uh and His Garbage Truck . . .

JOE

Not that one . . . he just blew this bird right apart, man . . . her eyes popped out and everything . . . out of sight . . .

CHARLEY

That was Skull Comics, man . . . no, Racist Pig Comics . . .

JOE

No, I know what it was . . . it was Fat Lip Funnies.

CHARLEY

Ohhh, *man* . . . I'm sorry . . . Louie took it last week. The fucker never brought it back . . .

JOE

What's this one like? Elephant Doodie?

CHARLEY

Nah, Wee-Wee Comics is better. Or Meatball. Look at this . . . Harry Kirschner . . . or Clumpy Morphus . . .

JOE

(*Picking up another one.*) . . . too *much* . . . Granny Crack-Baggy?

BRIGIT

(*Comes in again.*) Why don't you both just piss off?

CHARLEY

(*Gapes at her, then to* JOE.) Wassat? You seen that before?

JOE

Man . . . I never seen that before . . .

CHARLEY

(*Laughs.*) Wassat . . . 'f anybody pisses off, *you* piss off
. . . your presence here . . . is . . . uncalled for . . .

JOE

Un-called for . . . nun-called-for . . . balled for . . .

CHARLEY

Your . . . *type* is not called for . . . at the moment . . .
you are an un-called-for . . . type!

JOE

Don't call us . . . we'll call you . . .

BRIGIT

You shut up! Suppose I call the police and tell them you've
got hash up here?
   (*Both men explode into laughter.*)

JOE

Buzz buzz . . . here come de fuzz . . . fuzzl wuzzl
cuzzl . . .

CHARLEY

Buzza Buzza Buzza . . . here-a come-a fuzza . . . fuzz
. . . l fuzz . . . l . . . (*Calling.*) Haul in the foooore-
sail . . .

JOE

Land boooooooo!

CHARLEY

Hey . . . roll another one . . .

JOE

Right . . . one more for the *hiiiigh* road . . . once more
with *feeling* . . . (*Rips apart a cigarette for the tobacco,
mixes in the hash, rolls it up in a paper.*) I could stick it
down in the cigarette, man, but this is quicker . . . strong
this time, man . . . really strong . . . right? Hang on . . .

just a second . . . beautiful . . . beautiful . . . (JOE *lights up,* BRIGIT *grabs the joint and flings it away.* CHARLEY *picks it up.*)

CHARLEY
(*Lights it if necessary; if not, puffs ecstatically.*) Still alive, man . . .

JOE
(*To* BRIGIT.) You flipped? What's the matter with you? Cunt!
(BRIGIT *slaps him.*)

CHARLEY
You're flipping out!

BRIGIT
You're the ones who are flipping out! (*Tries to open the window.*) Fucking hashheads . . .

CHARLEY
Ah-ah-ah-ah . . . that stays shut . . . (*Stops her.*) That just stays shut . . .

BRIGIT
I can't breathe in here!

CHARLEY
Then fuck off!

BRIGIT
All right . . . (*Goes to the telephone, dials a number.*)

JOE
(*Sings.*) Ah'm gonna *get*cha on the *tel*-e-phone . . . Ain't never *gon*na letcha *be* a-lone . . .

BRIGIT
Will you shut *up?*

JOE
(*Nasal voice.*) What is your number, please? May I have your number, please?

CHARLEY
Darling! I love you!

JOE
No! Think of Cynthia! (*Picks up a* Playboy *and opens the gatefold.*)

CHARLEY
(*Tragically covering his eyes.*) She knows! Everything!

JOE
(*Back of fist against forehead.*) No! My God! No!

BRIGIT
Hello?

CHARLEY
I tell you she knows! She *knows!*

JOE
Aaaaaaaaaaaggggghhh! (*Falls on his face.*)

BRIGIT
Hello? (*To the others.*) Will you please shut *up?*
(*Both of them, grunting their buzz-fuzz Indian rhythm, dance in a circle.* BRIGIT *hangs up and dials another number.*)

JOE
Man, I'm blowing my mind . . . flying, man, flying . . .

CHARLEY
Moi aussi . . .
(*They imitate planes, buzzing* BRIGIT. *Then a silence falls.*)

JOE

(*Picks up a newspaper, rolls it into a long cylinder, moans.*)
Cynthia, Cynthia, I can't get you out of my mind! (*Holds
the cylinder like an erect penis.*)

CHARLEY

Forget her . . . you mad fool!

JOE

I'll try, by God, I'll try! (*The newspaper cylinder, which
he has held erect, now droops.*)

CHARLEY

That's the way! That's the way! (*Erects his own cylinder.*)

JOE

You bloody swine! *You* want her!

CHARLEY

You, my darling! I want *you!*

BRIGIT

(*Hangs up, dials another number.*) You bastards think
you're only playing.

CHARLEY

(*Gets the pillow from the bed, holds it at his crotch.*) Likey
likey . . . nice lady fucky fucky?

BRIGIT

Piss off!

JOE

Ooom ooom, baby . . . ooom ooom . . .

CHARLEY

Hare krishna . . . oom oom . . . hare hare . . .
oom . . .

JOE

Nice lady . . . nice lady . . . oom . . . oom . . .

CHARLEY

Nice lady jigajig . . . fucky fucky?
(*They crowd close to* BRIGIT, *who is having no success
with the phone.*)

BRIGIT

Fuck *off!*

CHARLEY

Suck off? Sweet *heart!*
(BRIGIT *knees him in the crotch. He doubles up and rolls
on the floor.*)

BRIGIT

(*Mincing voice.*) Oooooo . . . does it *hurt?*
(JOE *comes forward with a chair like a lion tamer, pushing* BRIGIT.)

BRIGIT

Stop it!

JOE

(*Pushing harder.*) Back, boy, back!

BRIGIT

Stop it, I said! (*Takes hold of the chair and pushes back.*)
(CHARLEY *puts on another record, fairly loud, then takes
the pillow and holds it in front of his crotch again. He
and* JOE *begin to dance around* BRIGIT, *each wielding his
respective weapon.* JOE *takes off his shirt,* CHARLEY *does
the same.*)

CHARLEY

(*To* BRIGIT, *who has left the phone.*) C'mon, you too . . .

JOE

Strip off . . . we'll all strip off . .
(*They keep dancing.*)

CHARLEY
You won't strip off?

JOE
I'm flying, man . . . flying out of *sight* . . .

BRIGIT
You start . . .

CHARLEY
(*Thumps her with the pillow, falls down himself.*)
Wooomp!

JOE
(*Tries to open* BRIGIT's *zipper, half succeeds.*) Hey, that
zipper sounds like my motor . . . wild . . . wild . . .
wild!

CHARLEY
(*Also tries, pulls the Levi's down a little.*) Verrr-y sexy . . .

BRIGIT
(*Pulls up the Levi's, goes for* CHARLEY, *who runs away, giggling like a little girl.*) Chickenshit! (JOE *shoves her with
the chair from behind, she goes for him in turn, and he runs
away giggling.* CHARLEY *gooses her with the champagne
bottle.*) *Damn* you!
    (*She throws something at his head, as* JOE *tries to get her
Levi's down again. She shoves him away, he falls on the
bed and she is about to thump him when* CHARLEY *shoves
her onto the bed. All three jump up again. She throws
herself at* JOE *but falls on the floor and he jumps on her.*)

CHARLEY
Gotcha!

JOE
(*Holding her hands behind her back, in a high voice.*) Police! Police! Police!

CHARLEY
Release, release, release! (BRIGIT *gets up.*) And now . . .
strip off! (*She grabs her bag and makes a dash for the door,
but he is there first, blocking the way, crooning in a Mexican accent.*) Hey, leetle *gor*-orl, I *want* to *show* you *some*-theeng . . .

BRIGIT
Fuck off! (Tries to force him out of the way.)

JOE
Hey, leetle *gor*-orl . . . we *love* you . . . (*Grabs her
breasts from behind. She twists away from him, kicking and
missing, tearful with fury.*)

CHARLEY
(*Struggles with her hand to hand, then pushes her away,
so that she stands between him and* JOE.) Doooon't be
afraaaiid, leetle gorl . . .

BRIGIT
(*Gasping and sobbing.*) You chickenshits . . .

JOE
(*Imitating a chicken.*) Fuuuu*uck*fuckfuckfuckfuckfuck-
fuck . . .

CHARLEY
(*Wielding a jacket like a cape.*) Toro! Toro!

JOE
Huuuh! Huuuuuh! (*Giggles. Both harry her, trying to get
her to charge, using jackets like capes, grunting and shouting "Toro," Toro" ad lib. She dodges away from them and
goes to the phone, dialing.*)

CHARLEY
(*Pinches her from behind.*) Who are you *cal*-leeng, leetle
gor-orl?

JOE

Buzz buzz the fuzz?

CHARLEY

Here come de fuzzluzzl?

JOE

(*Loudly*.) Toro!

BRIGIT

(*Jumps with fright.* CHARLEY *rips the receiver from her hand. There is a scuffle*.) I'll scream! (*She screams, he lets her go. She tries the door again, but* CHARLEY *stops her*.)

CHARLEY

Huuuuh! Toro, toro!

JOE

I *theenk* the *bool* he ees *not* very *brave, ami*-go . . .
    (BRIGHT *is nearly hysterical*.)

CHARLEY

The *bool* I *theenk* he *fancy* me, a*migo* . . .

JOE

Also I *theenk* I'm *fancying* the *bool* . . .
    (*He has picked up a stool. Both make mooing and bleating noises, shoving* BRIGIT *one way and then the other,* JOE *with his stool and* CHARLEY *with the pillow. An extra hard shove from* JOE's *stool sends her reeling past* CHARLEY *to fall into the debris near the window. She comes up weeping hysterically and holding a kitchen knife*.)

JOE

Hey a*migo* . . . the *bool* he *have* one *horn* . . .

BRIGIT

(*Screams desperately*.) Get away from me! (*Tries to make the door again, but is driven back, unmercifully harassed with pillows, which the boys wield like muletas*.)

CHARLEY
Huuuh, huuuh, toro . . . toro . . .

JOE
Hey . . . *toro!* (*Whacks her on the bum with his pillow.*)

CHARLEY
(*As* BRIGIT *turns to face* JOE, *whacks her in turn with a pillow.*) Hey, toro!

JOE
(*Repeating the trick.*) Toro, toro!
(*They begin to pound her with the pillows, forgetting
that she has the knife. The pounding increases in tempo
as they laugh and shout to each other.*)

CHARLEY
Hey, a*m*igo, the *bool* he ees *chee*cken . . .

JOE
He *don'* like to *fight,* I *thee*-eenk!
(*Shouting, whooping, they close in on her, pounding
with the pillows until the three of them are entangled
in a general shoving, shouting, pounding, struggling
melee. Suddenly* BRIGIT'*s hysterical scream cuts through
the yelling and uproar.*)

BRIGIT
GET AWAY FROM MEEEEEEEEE!
(*They all stumble together in a flurry of pillows and
floundering, confused arms and heads.* JOE *staggers back
with his face against the wardrobe while* CHARLEY *reels
onto the bed, laughing helplessly.* BRIGIT *stands still, her
hysteria suddenly gone, icily calm. She watches* JOE.)

CHARLEY
(*Doubled up.*) Hey, a*miii*go, the *bool* he ees *fee*nesh, I
*thee*nk . . . (*Something about* BRIGIT *makes him stop*

laughing and look at JOE. JOE *turns from the wardrobe, not too slowly, moving convulsively. The knife protrudes from his chest and blood pours down the front of him, soaking all the front of his shirt and pants.*)

CHARLEY
(*Numb.*) No . . .

JOE
(*Staggers toward* CHARLEY.) Char . . . ley . . . (*Sinks down, dies at* BRIGIT's *feet.*)

CHARLEY
(*Still numb, plunges forward almost automatically as* JOE *sinks, catches his hand. As he holds the hand,* BRIGIT *sits calmly on the bed.*) Joe . . . Joe? What'd you do? Joe? (*Still numb, looks at* BRIGIT.) What'd you do? . . . You flipped . . . you flipped . . . no . . . no, you flipped . . . I mean . . . what am I gonna do . . . I mean . . . (*Drops the hand in horror and stands up, backing away.*) Is he dead? Hey, is he dead? Hey, you think he's dead? (*Watches dumbly as* BRIGIT *goes to the phone, then decides not to call.*) He's *dead* . . .

BRIGIT
(*Icily.*) It was self-defense.

CHARLEY
Yeah . . . yeah, right . . . I mean . . . you flipped . . . uh . . . uh . . . God, I . . . man, I'm still stoned . . . it's all . . . all . . . I mean . . . what are you gonna do? I mean, you've gotta *do* something . . . I mean, I'm . . . stoned, right? what . . . what are we gonna do? . . . Christ, what if someone comes . . . can you look at him? *Please?*

BRIGIT
Stop it.

CHARLEY

He's dead . . . listen, baby, you . . . you flipped your mind . . . you flipped your mind . . . listen, someone might come . . . somebody might come . . . I mean, just think if somebody comes . . .

BRIGIT

(*Goes to* JOE, *picks up his hand, feels for a pulse.*) Yes, he's dead. (*She is cool and calm.*)

CHARLEY

No . . . not really . . . listen, really? (*Cringes in a corner.*) Man, I'm . . . flipping out . . . I'm flipping out . . . listen . . . what are we gonna do?

BRIGIT

(*Calmly.*) Nothing. It was self-defense. He tried to rape me.

CHARLEY

I mean . . . I mean . . . I mean . . . you flipped . . . no! (*Disoriented, moves around.* BRIGIT *puts on "Play with Fire" by the Stones, lights a cigarette.*)

CHARLEY

Hey, I . . . I feel funny . . . I feel really funny . . . hey . . . turn down the record . . . please, turn down the record . . .

BRIGIT

(*Warm, friendly.*) Come on . . .

CHARLEY

Listen, if somebody hears it . . .

BRIGIT

(*Removing her Levi's and T shirt.*) Come on . . . (*She is left wearing briefs.*)

CHARLEY

What . . . whatsa matter . . . what're you doing that for?
(*She turns down the lights, then lights a candle.*)

BRIGIT

(*Soft but excited.*) Come *on* . . . (*Goes to him, opens his
shirt, pulling him toward the bed. Some afternoon light
comes through the closed shutters.*)

CHARLEY

(*Dazed.*) What're you doing . . .

BRIGIT

(*Voice thick with excitement.*) Don't you like me any
more? (*Pulls him down onto the bed, tries to get him to
pull down the briefs.*)

CHARLEY

(*Whimpering.*) I can't do that . . . (*Collapses on his knees
at the side of the bed, puts his head on her knee, clutches
at her leg like a child.*)

BRIGIT

(*Pushing him violently aside, stands up angrily, and turns
on the light.*) Christ!

CHARLEY

(*Dreamily.*) We gonna go now?
   (BRIGIT *is calmly getting dressed again.*)

CHARLEY

(*Stumbles around the room, finds a small rug and rolls* JOE's
body in it, then pulls it behind the bed.) Hey . . . you
won't tell anybody we were smoking . . . you know? . . .
(*Starts violently.*) Somebody coming . . . (*Plunges to the
door.*) Didn't you hear . . . hey? . . .

BRIGIT

(*Takes the car key from* JOE's *jacket and goes to the door, where* CHARLEY *cringes.*) Get out of the way. I'm going now.

CHARLEY
(*Clutches at her.*) Where you going?

BRIGIT
(*Pries his hands loose.*) Will you let *go*, please?

CHARLEY
(*Coming apart.*) No . . . don't go . . . I mean . . . they'll see you . . . I mean, they'll get you . . . wait . . . just wait'll I come down . . .
  (BRIGIT *coldly pushes him aside and goes.*)

CHARLEY
(*As the door closes in his face.*) No, wait . . . wait . . .
  (*Too frightened to open the door, he stumbles back across the room, shambles about, finds himself staring down at the body. The car starts up outside, pulls away. He sits down, starts up in panic, listens at the door, goes to the window and listens, lurches to the wardrobe and climbs in, shutting the door. A pause. The phone rings. After five rings* CHARLEY *slinks out of the wardrobe and lifts the receiver without saying anything. Then he whispers.*)
Who . . . oh . . . Monika . . . (*Very softly.*) Joe? Uh he left already . . . I dunno . . . you can't hear me? (*Still softly.*) No, really . . . he's not here . . . maybe . . . he went to the movies . . . (*Obviously wanting to end the conversation.*) Yeah . . . yeah, I'll tell him . . . yeah . . . yeah . . . right . . . bye . . . (*Hangs up and tiptoes back to the wardrobe to shut himself in.*)

BLACKOUT

PARTY FOR SIX

English Version by
Renata and Martin Esslin

Characters

FERDY
FRED
FLOSSIE
FRANK
FANNY
FREDA
LANDLORD

(The action takes place in a medium-sized town with a red-brick university.)

SCENE ONE

(*Entrance Hall. Open door to Lounge on left. Door to passage upstage. In the center of the floor a large, heavy carpet. A ceiling light, bright and cold when lit up. In the corner upstage-right, a hat-and-coat stand. On the wall right a cupboard with built-in drinks cabinet. Between cupboard and hat-and-coat stand an old discarded divan, gray and shabby.*)

(*When the curtain rises the Hall is almost in darkness. The only source of light is through the open Lounge door. Sound of pop records and clinking of glasses from the Lounge.* FERDY, *a student aged twenty, enters from the Lounge, turns on the light in the Hall, goes to the drinks cabinet, takes out some bottles of wine, turns the light off, and disappears back into the Lounge, clinking his bottles. He returns, turns on the light, takes a bunch of keys from a hook by the door to passage at back, and goes out into the passage. The stage remains lit. After some time he enters from back. Sound of water flushing in a lavatory. He turns off the light, goes into the Lounge, and closes the door. The stage is now in complete darkness. In the Lounge* FERDY *puts on another record: "Come Prima." It is heard softly through the door. Doorbell.* FERDY *enters from Lounge, turns on light, goes through door to passage, and, outside, opens another door. Voices:*)

FERDY

Hi.

FRED

Hello there.

FERDY

Come on in.

FRED

Anyone here yet?

FERDY

No, you're the first.
       (*They enter Hall.*) Got the brandy?

FRED

Yeah. I've got some. Pinched it from my old lady.

FERDY

Great.

FRED

I could have got some more . . . but . . .

FERDY

(*Disappearing into the Lounge.*) Take your things off. Just
going to bung on another record.

FRED

(*Takes off his coat, puts bottle on divan.*) Hey! Ferdy!
Ferdy!

FERDY

(*Putting on record.*) Yeah? What's up?

FRED

Is Frank going to bring some booze too?

FERDY

He said he would.

FRED
Is Fanny coming?

FERDY
Shut up. Listen to my new record.

FRED
Is Fanny coming?

FERDY
(*Entering from Lounge.*) Listen to that record. (*Sings.*) "If I had" . . .

FRED
Hey! Is Fanny coming?

FERDY
(*His attention on record.*) Yeah. Sure. Come on inside. Leave the booze there for now. We'll kick off with beer. (*Both go into the room.* FERDY *turns off the light in the Hall.* FRED *is about to close the door* . . . *only their voices are heard.*)

FERDY
Leave the door open. Or we won't hear the bell. Great record, isn't it?

FRED
Not bad.

FERDY
Bought it yesterday. (*They appear to be listening to record as nothing else is heard. When the record finishes:*)

FRED
Is it true that Frank has taken up with Fanny?

FERDY
That's what he says. But I think . . .

FRED

I always thought it's no go with her.

FERDY

On the contrary. If you give her the right soft soap, you're in clover with her. But I don't know if Frank . . .

FRED

That's what I mean.

FERDY

I don't believe it. Anyway. You got your eye on her?

FRED

What do you mean, got my eye on her. I was just wondering. Might have a bit of a go tonight.

FERDY

What about Flossie?

FRED

Don't you want her?

FERDY

I don't want anybody in particular. I'll make do with Fanny if necessary.

FRED

And Frank?

FERDY

He can have Freda. (*Laughs.*)

FRED

You don't know Frank.

FERDY

It'll sort itself out. Wait and see.
    (*Doorbell is rung repeatedly.*) I'll go. Put on a good record. (FERDY *enters Hall and turns on the light.* FRED *puts*

on the same record as before. FERDY *out to passage and opens the door. Voices:)*

FERDY
In you come!

FLOSSIE
Hi.

FERDY
Hi there!

FRANK
Hello. Anybody here yet?

FERDY
No. *(Enters.)* Come on in. Close the door after you, please. Freddie's here.

FRED
(From Lounge.) Hello!

FRANK
Hi, mate!

FRED
How's the old boozer?

FERDY
Take your things off.

FLOSSIE
(FERDY *takes her coat.)* Thanks. (FRANK *has taken his coat off and goes into the Lounge.)* Got a mirror somewhere?

FRANK
(In Lounge.) Hello.

FERDY
You look smashing as you are. (FLOSSIE *giggles.)* Come on. *(They go into the Lounge.* FERDY *turns off light in the Hall.*

The door remains open and some light falls into the Hall. Their voices only:)

FLOSSIE

(*Apparently to* FRED.) Hello.

FERDY

Have you heard this record?

FRANK

This one?

FERDY

Hang on. I'll play it again.

FRED

Play something else. We can have it after.

FERDY

No. Hang on. Just a second.

FLOSSIE

I'd like to hear this one.

FERDY

This one?

FLOSSIE

Or this.

FERDY

Oh, wait a minute. Let's play this one first. Then you can play what you like. (*Puts on record, turns volume right up. Sings.*)

FRED

Turn it down a bit! (*Volume very low.*)

FLOSSIE

I thought Freda and Fanny would be here . . .

FERDY

Well, as you see . . .

FLOSSIE

Am I the only female here then? . . . (*Smiles audibly.*)

FRED

(*Slily.*) So far! So far . . . let's hope . . . let's hope some more will turn up! (*Laughs. Long pause. Very long pause. Then someone—*FRANK*—closes the door. The stage is plunged in darkness and all is quiet. After some time the door is opened.*)

FERDY

Just in case. So we can hear the bell. (*Pause.*)

FLOSSIE

I wonder where they've got to.

FRED

All in good time.

FRANK

(*Laughs a little.*) Good time—you don't say!

FLOSSIE

D'you mind if I help myself to one of these?

FERDY

Help yourself! Have some eats while it's there. (*Pause while they eat.*)

FRANK

What's that?

FERDY

I don't know. It all came in a packet.

FLOSSIE

It's a bit like . . . what d'you call it . . . a cheese straw.

FERDY
There's cheese in it.

FRED
Not bad. (FRANK *goes to door and into the dark Hall.*)

FRANK
Where's the light?

FERDY
(*Calls from the room.*) To the right of the door. To the right.
(FRANK *turns on light.*)

FRANK
Is there a key?

FERDY
No. By the other door. There's a whole bunch of them.

FRANK
Got it. (*Goes out to passage, leaves light on in Hall.*)

FRED
How about opening one of these bottles?

FERDY
Shouldn't we wait until everyone's here?

FLOSSIE
I don't mind. I don't really want a drink.

FRED
I wouldn't mind a beer.

FERDY
Help yourself if you want some . . .
(*Sound of bottles.*)

FRED
Got a bottle opener?

FERDY

Isn't there one there? (*Pause.*)

FRED

Can't see one.

FERDY

(*Enters Hall and goes to drinks cabinet, searches, muttering.*) Shit . . . where's the bottle opener? (*Finds one. Goes back into Lounge, leaves light on in Hall.*) Here you are!

FRED

Thanks. (*Sound of bottle being opened.*) Shall I open another one?

FERDY

Not for me.

FRED

What about you?

FLOSSIE

No, thanks. I'll just have a nibble.

FERDY

Good, aren't they?

FLOSSIE

Super. Where did you get them?

FERDY

I don't know what the place is called. At the top of Market Street.

FLOSSIE

Keen's?

FERDY

Where's that?

FLOSSIE
Next to Horne's.

FERDY
Where's Horne's?

FRED
Opposite the stamp shop.

FERDY
Yeah, that's it. Yeah.

FLOSSIE
That's where I do my shopping. (FRANK *comes back into the Hall. Sound of water flushing.*)

FRANK
Shall I turn the light off?

FERDY
Yes, turn it off. (FRANK *turns off light, goes into Lounge, closes the door, opens it again at once.*)

FRANK
You having a beer?

FERDY
Like one?

FRANK
What a question. Let's have it. Now we're away! (FRED *laughs in agreement.*)

FERDY
Great minds think alike, eh?

FRANK
Cheers.

FRED

Bottoms up! (*Soon both exclaim with exaggerated delight:* "*Aaahhhh!*")

FERDY

I think I'll have one too. What have you done with the bottle opener?

FRED

Here you are. (*Doorbell.*)

FLOSSIE

That'll be them.

FERDY

I'll go . . . (*Enters Hall, turns on light, goes out to passage. Voices:*)
  (FERDY *makes sound of a fanfare. Opens door.* FANNY *and* FREDA *laugh.*)
Hello to you!

FANNY

Hello to you, he says! (*Laughs.*)

FREDA

Are we last?

FERDY

Yeah. (*Shows them in.*) Come on in! (*Someone puts on a new record in the Lounge. Volume fairly high.*) Take your coats off! (*He takes coats.* FLOSSIE *enters from Lounge.*)

FLOSSIE

Hello.

FREDA

Hello, Flossie.

FANNY

Been here long?

FLOSSIE
No, I've only just come.

FANNY
Christ! I think I've left my comb behind!

FLOSSIE
You don't need one.

FERDY
You look smashing as you are.

FREDA
(*Whispers to* FERDY.) Where's the loo?

CURTAIN

SCENE TWO

(*The same as in Scene One. The Hall is lit up. The door to the Lounge is closed, music is heard from inside.* FRED *is standing in the Hall, he looks undecided as if waiting for something. Outside, the lavatory is flushed.* FANNY *enters, hangs up the key on the hook by the passage door.* FRED *quickly moves up to her from behind, embraces her, and kisses the back of her neck. She struggles free.*)

FANNY
Mind my dress.

FRED
Don't go.

FANNY
What do you want? (FRED *gives her a juicy kiss.*) Ha! (FANNY *goes into Lounge and closes the door after her.* FRED *takes the bunch of keys and goes out through door to passage. He is somewhat tipsy. For a time the Hall remains empty. Then:*)

FERDY
(*Looking out from Lounge.*) Freddie? Freddie?

FRED
(*Muffled.*) Engaged.

FERDY
(*Into Lounge.*) (*Laughs.*) Engaged! (*Laughter rings out from the Lounge,* FERDY *closes the door.*)

FRED

(*Sings.*) Lalala, lalala, lalala! A-hunting we will go . . .
Lalala, lalala, lalala . . . (*Flushes.*)
   (FRED *enters Hall, hangs up keys, goes to Lounge door,
   and listens. He turns off the light, and turns it on again.
   On, off, on, off. Nearly twenty times. With the light on
   he knocks on the Lounge door. Several voices call: "Come
   in."* FRED *goes into the Lounge.*)

FLOSSIE

Oh, it's you?

FRED

Go on! You didn't expect me! (*Voices:*)

FERDY

Freda, put on a twist record!

FRANK

Twist Twist, Twist, Twist!

FERDY

Shut the door, somebody! (*The door is slammed shut, the
stage remains lit up and empty. The sound of the music is
low. Gradually it increases. The noise of the party in the
Lounge reaches its climax. Laughter. Doorbell. The noise
in the Lounge stops.* FERDY *opens the door. Voices:*)

FLOSSIE

I didn't hear anything.

FRANK

I thought I did. (*Doorbell is rung again.*)

FANNY

I expect it's the landlord. (FERDY *crosses Hall and goes out
into the passage. He opens the door. Voices:*)

FERDY

Good evening.

LANDLORD

Tell me, Mr. P., have you got a zoo full of monkeys in there?

(*Laughter from the Lounge.*)

FERDY

No.

LANDLORD

That's what it sounds like. I think the whole house is coming down. It is quite unbearable.

FERDY

I do apologize. We'll be quiet in a minute. You know, we've got a little party going . . .

LANDLORD

Okay. I've got nothing against parties. But you don't have to go stamping around all the time.

FERDY

No, no. That was only just now. We were playing a game of forfeits, you know. And we got a bit carried away.

LANDLORD

All right, all right. But try and keep it bearable—please.

FERDY

Cheerio!

LANDLORD

Good night. (FERDY *closes the door.*)

FERDY

(*In the Hall.*) Carry on, everybody. (*Goes back into the Lounge.*) No need for restraint. The landlord is quite sympathetic.

FRED

You don't say!

FREDA

Yeah! (*The door remains slightly ajar.*)

FRANK

Anybody got a fag? (*Several voices: "No."*)

FANNY

I may have some in my coat pocket.

FRANK

Mind if I get them?

FANNY

Go ahead, in the left inside pocket.
(FRANK *goes into the Hall and to coat stand. He looks through pockets.*)

FRANK

Where?

FANNY

The left inside pocket, or on the right outside.
(FRANK *searches.*)

FRANK

Not a thing! (*Goes back to Lounge door.*) You have a look.

FANNY

Oh, men are hopeless . . .
(*Goes into the Hall and toward coat stand.* FRANK *closes Lounge door and turns the light off. For a short time nothing is seen or heard. Then heavy breathing. The Lounge door is opened abruptly.* FLOSSIE *looks into the Hall and turns on the light.*)

FLOSSIE

I beg your pardon! (*They are sitting on the divan, somewhat embarrassed, but nothing much seems to have happened.* FLOSSIE *closes the door and turns the light off.*)

FANNY

Come on. Let's get back inside.

FRANK

Wait a bit. They want to be alone too.

FANNY

Come on. (FANNY *turns on the light, straightens her hair.*
FRANK *remains seated on the divan.*) Come on, now.
(FANNY *goes back into the Lounge,* FRANK *lies down on
the divan. The Lounge door is slammed, the light stays
on,* FRANK *closes his eyes. Soon the Lounge door is opened
abruptly.*)

FERDY

There he is!

FRED

He's asleep.

FREDA

Frankie! Frankie! Wakey-wakey!

FRANK

Turn off that bloody light!
(*They turn it off, return to the Lounge, and close the
door. For some time everything is quiet, then the Lounge
door is opened again.* FRED *enters carrying a glass full of
wine, turns on the light, goes over to the divan, and pours
the wine over* FRANK'S *face.*)

FRANK

Bloody bastard! (*He does not move.* FRED *runs back into
the Lounge, giggling and somewhat frightened, and locks
the door from inside.*)

CURTAIN

SCENE THREE

(The same. The Hall is brightly lit. FRANK *is sleeping on the divan. The three girls' coats and* FRED's *duffel coat are gone from the hat- and coat-stand. The Lounge door is half open. For a long time there is no action. Then— somewhere, far away, the noise of goods wagons being shunted in a railway yard. Then silence. Sound of shunting is repeated at regular intervals—30 seconds. After four minutes—)*

CURTAIN

SCENE FOUR

(*The same. The Hall is brightly lit and empty. All doors are wide open.* FANNY *enters from the passage, wearing overalls. She is carrying clean glasses, which she replaces in the drinks cabinet.*)

FANNY

Not one of them broken. (*Sound of vacuum cleaner from the Lounge.*) It takes twice as long as the party itself to clear up afterward! (*Goes back into the passage.*)

FLOSSIE

It's not too bad. (*Continues to Hoover Lounge.* FANNY *returns to the Hall carrying two clean plates. She stops in the center of the Hall, smiles in the direction of the Lounge, and calls out.*)

FANNY

Frank caught it bad last night!

FLOSSIE

(*Above vacuum cleaner.*) And how! (FANNY *puts plates into drinks cabinet.*)

CURTAIN